PETERBOROUGH COURT

PETERBOROUGH COURT

THE STORY OF

The Daily Telegraph

by

LORD BURNHAM

with 12 *pages of half-tone illustrations*

CASSELL & COMPANY LTD
LONDON

CASSELL & CO. LTD.
37/38 St. Andrew's Hill, Queen Victoria Street,
London, E.C.4
and at

31/34 *George IV Bridge, Edinburgh;* 210 *Queen Street, Melbourne,*
26/30 *Clarence Street, Sydney; Uhlmann Road, Hawthorne, Brisbane;*
C.P.O. 3031, *Auckland, N.Z.;* 1068 *Broadview Avenue, Toronto* 6;
P.O Box 275, *Cape Town; P.O. Box* 1386, *Salisbury, S. Rhodesia;*
Munsoor Building, Main Street, Colombo 11; *Haroon Chambers, South*
Napier Road, Karachi; 13/14 *Ajmeri Gate Extension, New Delhi* 1;
15 *Graham Road, Ballard Estate, Bombay* 1; 17 *Chittaranjan Avenue,*
Calcutta 13; *Avenida* 9 *de Julho* 1138; *São Paulo; Galeria Güemes,*
Escritorio 518/520 *Florida* 165, *Buenos Aires; P.O. Box* 959,
Accra, Gold Coast; 25 *rue Henri Barbusse, Paris* 5e; *Islands Brygge* 5,
Copenhagen

TO THE ARCHITECTS OF SUCCESS

EDWARD
LORD BURNHAM

WILLIAM
VISCOUNT CAMROSE

CONTENTS

ILLUSTRATIONS

AUTHOR'S NOTE

I HAVE found my task very difficult. The *Daily Telegraph* may have broken records, certainly it kept none and I have had to do my best with casual references in books by members of the staff, a few scrappy memoranda and letters, a fairly reliable memory, and the files of the newspaper itself.

This made impossible one model of a newspaper history, the kind that tells what went on behind the scenes. My grandfather for some reason kept several letters of Gladstone's asking him to dinner but no written record of the famous meeting after matins at the Temple Church or of any of their important conversations. Le Sage resolutely refused to keep any notes after their immediate importance had ceased and took care that no one else's record of anything that happened in the office was left for history. A method, adopted by another centenarian paper, of writing a short history of the times as illuminated by its columns, I have rejected, because if there are no good short histories of the last hundred years Arthur Bryant will surely write one better than I could.

And so I decided upon an impressionist sketch of the *Daily Telegraph* and of some of the men who made it.

I present my first and last book. For me it has been a labour of love and I hope it may interest others.

A BIOGRAPHICAL NOTE

Naturally during a hundred years the images of the sovereigns changed but so also did their superscriptions. This note is given to make clear their nomenclature in a story which is not given in strict chronological order.

Edward Lawson became a baronet in 1892, and in 1903 Lord Burnham. He was succeeded in the title and control of the paper in 1916 by his son, Harry Lawson, who was created a Viscount in 1919. (The author is the son of Harry's younger brother who was by profession a soldier and took no part in the paper.)

The *Daily Telegraph* was bought in 1927 by Sir William Berry (Viscount Camrose), Mr. Gomer Berry (Viscount Kemsley), and Sir Edward Iliffe (Lord Iliffe). The partnership was dissolved in 1937 and Lord Camrose took over sole control. Lord Camrose died in 1954, and his eldest son, Seymour, became Chairman of the *Daily Telegraph* and his second son, Michael, its Editor-in-Chief.

CHAPTER I

EARLY DAYS

THE reasons which induce men to found daily newspapers are many, some good, some bad. It may be simply to make money, it may be to support some economic theory or political party, it may even be a simple and honest desire to increase the fund of human knowledge of day-to-day events. Colonel Arthur Burroughes Sleigh started the *Daily Telegraph* in 1855 with a more definite and limited objective, to pursue a vendetta against the Duke of Cambridge, later Commander-in-Chief of the Army. History does not reveal the reason of the quarrel but from what is known of the gallant Colonel it may well be that on this occasion at least the Duke was in the right. Be that as it may, the paper failed to establish itself and was taken over in settlement of his bill and a loan by the printer, Mr. J. M. Levy, who decided to launch it with a wider purpose.

Mr. Levy was a printer in a fair way of business. He had the plant for the production of the paper but was short of the necessary working capital to redeem the initial failure. The needs of those days were moderate and Mr. Levy's ideas of the requisite amount were moderate even for those days. He decided to form the business as a partnership divided, as was the custom with ships, into sixty-four shares, and his first recourse was to his own family. He took a quarter of the shares himself, his son Edward took an eighth and his brother Lionel* a half. Lionel Lawson was the plutocrat of the family. At various times in his life he owned an ink factory in Paris, had an interest in the early diamond mines in South Africa and in theatres and was at one time the owner of the Gaiety Theatre, but in 1855 his financial position was only considerable in comparison with the rest of the family.

Two figures have been mentioned as the target for the would-be newspaper proprietors—£4,000 and £8,000, and almost certainly it was the lower amount. Whichever it was, they were short of the last eighth share which was finally provided by a gentleman named George Moss.

Mr. Robert Sievier, in a more than somewhat scurrilous article on Lord Burnham and the early days of the *Daily Telegraph* published in the *Winning Post* early in this century, described him as Pubby Moss and suggested that he was the licensee of an alehouse patronized by employees of the printing works. Sievier submitted the proof of the article to Lord Burnham in advance, but the purpose of submission seemed rather to secure modification of comment than verification of fact. Lord Burnham declined the suggestion with its possible implications, and so there is no confirmation of this description of Mr. Moss, but it is generally accepted that he was a wholly reputable person and at the time the machine manager of the printing works.

Whether from confidence or anxiety, the first step taken by the proprietors was to tie up the partnership arrangement so that no member of the family could dispose of his interest in the *Daily Telegraph* without the consent of all. This was done by a series of trusts so carefully devised and so intricate that they persisted

* Lionel Lawson Levy took his second name of Lawson for business purposes and later, in respect of a deed of gift from him his nephew, Edward, did the same.

2

beyond the sale by common consent of the partners to Lord Camrose and his associates and are an embarrassment to the Lawson family to this day. They could not of course tie up the outside element so completely, but as that element received for very many years an annual return of £15,500 for their share, whether the original capital was £500 or £1,000 there was little reason for complaint or temptation to change the investment.

Levy's works were in Shoe Lane where Peterborough Court made exit and there he printed the *Sunday Times* which then had a certain position but no magnitude. When, seventy-two years later, the *Daily Telegraph* passed out of his family it went to Sir William Berry who needed a companion for the *Sunday Times*. The ground of Peterborough Court, once the site of the London hostel of the Abbots of Peterborough, was soon to be completely covered by the office and works of the *Daily Telegraph*. The *Daily Telegraph* publishing office remained on the north side of the Strand between St. Clement Danes Church and Temple Bar until 1860.

The working capital may have been small but expenses were not very great in those days. A compositor's average earnings were about three pounds a week, high compared to other workers but a fifth of what they are to-day, and a web machine cost about £600 and produced about 7,000 copies an hour. To-day one rotary unit and folder, printing an eight-page paper, with its electrical equipment would cost £15,000.

The editorial staff was neither extensive nor expensive. Le Sage in 1863 started as personal assistant to Edward Lawson at a salary of three guineas a week, eighteen years later Hall Richardson joined the staff at the same rate, and Edward Blanchard in the sixties got £150 a year as dramatic critic. It would be a mistake, however, to think that *Daily Telegraph* salaries were not in accordance with

3

the general level of the day. In 1865 James Macintyre became assistant editor at a salary of two hundred and fifty pounds a year, which was fifty pounds better than he was offered for a similar post on the *Scotsman*.

Reporters and sub-editors were recruited as now from provincial and local papers and, as now, left them to better themselves. In a letter of advice to Hall Richardson, Edward Russell, Editor of the *Liverpool Post*, says that his first editorship was that of the *Islington Gazette*, a successful local paper, for which he was paid £1 15s. 6d. a week.

Leader writers, special writers, and foreign correspondents were of course paid more, but not extravagantly. It was generally said that Sala ' received the salary of an ambassador ' which may well have been so, though almost the only record of Sala remaining in the office is a file of short letters all addressed to J. M. Levy, identical in subject, and only varying in the amount requested as an advance of salary. He might well have kept the matter in type leaving only the figures to be filled in with his meticulous handwriting. Usually it was ten pounds, which hardly suggests an ambassadorial scale.

Though quite early in its history the *Telegraph* went large on special reporters and writers, the inside staff was very modest. Macintyre records that he was pleasantly untroubled by details as ' there were as many as three sub-editors '. Newsprint, the chief raw material, now £55, was £14 14s. a ton of which threepence per pound was the paper duty.

Though expenses may have been low, revenue was indeed slight. The end of the stamp duty of a penny a copy encouraged Colonel Sleigh to bring out his paper at twopence a copy against the prevailing price of fivepence, a step which was considered the height of folly, and no surprise was caused by its failure.

4

Completely undeterred, his successors, regardless of their meagre working capital and almost imperceptible advertising revenue (the first day's takings over the counter were seven shillings and sixpence), reduced the price of the sixty-ninth issue to one penny. For a bad debt they had taken over a newspaper with a slender good will, infinitesimal circulation, and a contract with Thornton Hunt, son of Leigh Hunt of the *Examiner*, essayist, poet, critic, and enemy of the Prince Regent. The last acquisition was certainly an asset though terminable at a month's notice, and the only other that they had was their own courage.

Conditions in England were not particularly favourable. Palmerston was in power with a majority of thirteen. True, income tax was only one and twopence in the pound but that was considered intolerably high. The Crimean War was pursuing its uninspired and uninspiring course and contrary to public belief wars are not financially good times for newspapers.

There was undoubtedly a field for a new paper, particularly if it were cheap and well distributed. The provincial daily Press hardly existed before the repeal of the stamp tax in June, 1855. In London there were ten papers, *The Times* at sevenpence and the *Standard*, *Daily News*, *Morning Post*, and the rest at fivepence. In 1840 their total circulation was 49,000, of which 10,000 was the figure for *The Times*. In 1846 the *Daily News* at the end of its first six weeks had only 4,000 circulation and all Dilke's price cutting only raised it to 22,000 before it came back to fivepence.

Let us take a look at the first penny newspaper in this country, promising to be, when support from the public enabled its size to be increased, ' the largest, best, and cheapest newspaper in the world '.

The editorial 'we', after taking full credit for their rôle as champions of the people and advocates of measures of general progress which they believe to be for the good of the people, get into full swing.

There is no reason why a daily newspaper conducted with high tone, should not be produced at a price which will place it within the means of all classes of the community. The extension of the circulation of such a journal must prove beneficial to the public at large. If artisan and Peer can alike peruse daily the same wholesome literary matter, produced by first-class writers, the general tone of society must benefit. The working man will feel assured that we consider that he is deserving of having laid before him a newspaper compiled with a care which places it in the Hamlet and secures its perusal in the Palace.

It will be noted that the high democratic purpose, typographically impaired by the treatment of Peer and artisan, is restored by giving capitals to both Hamlet and Palace.

In hamlet and palace there was, to use modern jargon, appreciable consumer resistance, but in the large number of ordinary houses, in which the so-called middle class lived, the *Daily Telegraph* soon made headway. Within a week of the reduction of price it claimed a higher circulation than any London morning newspaper except *The Times*. The first figure given was 27,000 copies in January, 1856. The *Telegraph* was described by Edmund Yates as the paper of the man on the knifeboard of the omnibus. The Palace was not won from *The Times*, the hamlet was waiting for Harmsworth, but of all that lay between the *Daily Telegraph* was indisputably monarch. In the meantime the proprietors, and possibly their bankers, had some anxious moments.

True that by the end of 1855 the advertisement columns had risen from three to six and the advertisement rates had been raised, but only to sixpence a line for general advertisements and ninepence a line for public companies, an average of about £5 a column and

6

£30 for the total advertisement revenue of each issue. Only occasionally did an advertiser take such considerable space as one trader who took a very rosy view of the coverage of the *Daily Telegraph* :

> The *Telegraph* and *Courier*
> While kept in active mood
> Is just the kind of messenger
> To work for Underwood
> For where a *Courier* can run
> A *Telegraph* will be
> And thus all nations neath the sun
> Will hear of First-Class Tea.

The *Telegraph* may not have spread as widely as Mr. Underwood thought but he could hardly complain of the advertising rates for a circulation claimed to be greater than any four morning papers together, excluding *The Times*.

In the third year, small drawings of ships in the shipping advertisements give an encouragement to advertisers to take larger spaces and indeed are the very faint beginnings of display advertising.

Intensive salesmanship was then unknown and the proprietors need not be given undue credit for their appreciation of the fact that a good newspaper sells itself and that the first thing to do was to get the content right. And this had their most careful consideration. It is interesting to have a look at some extracts from a long memorandum from Thornton Hunt to the proprietors.

> The main object of this memorandum is to consider how the success of the D.T. can be protected against a competition which looks in some degree formidable. I rely strongly on two principles. The first is that a belief in the disproportionate increase of success in other papers will tend to bring about the success of those others. The second is, that any success which is not in one way or other

progressive and constantly on the increase, will not continue but will decline and cease.

Hunt seems to consider the *Daily News* as the most dangerous competitor. He attributes this in part to its firm hold with a radical minority but he goes on to say 'the success of the *Daily News* is chiefly brought about by the larger proportion of space given to news and by the more effective supply of news, especially in foreign departments'. He concludes his survey of the *Daily News* with 'we cannot correct the effect without *more* than recovering the lost ground' and then goes on to some constructive suggestions :

> We are only now at the beginning of a new era in science and let us not forget that science is to be taught in every school. Our policy should be one of making the leading daily paper take the lead also in that department of general yet special intelligence. We should report all striking events in science, so told that the intelligent public can understand what has happened and can see its bearing on our daily life and our future. The same principle should apply to all other events—to fashion, to new inventions, to new methods of conducting business.
>
> There also wants more technical certainty in dealing with particular subjects. A paper of high authority should always have at command such men as can write with correctness, certainty, distinct force and authority on military, on naval affairs, on law; also at least one writer who can with the same authority handle subjects of official statement—can do it accurately, in suitable language with an air of authority.

After nearly a century I have heard Lord Camrose somewhat more succinctly enunciate many of these principles.

In most newspapers of the day the field of news covered was very limited and the *Daily Telegraph* set out to extend it. A notice is published in the paper in its second year directed to provincial reporters and offering liberal payment for any material which they may submit. In the same year an office was set up in Paris and soon a regular daily column from Paris made its appearance dealing with everything from politics and the personalities behind politics to fashion, the theatre, and Parisian gossip and scandal. At the end of 1857 there was a regular weekly letter from Toronto. There was also the occasional semi-news feature article such as one bearing the curious heading ' Steam Intercourse with Australia '.

Though the field of news in journals may have been limited they contained little else. The *Telegraph* proprietors realized that if there was a public for them it was an entirely new public who never saw the weeklies and monthlies, which catered for the special interests of the educated man and woman. They sensed, possibly more instinctively than from any close reasoning, the effect of the development of education on a growing population. As early as September 19th, 1855, the first book reviews were published in the paper and on October 27th the first dramatic criticism. Soon, books of special interest received long critical notices. Music also received special attention, and sport.

Instinctive or reasoned, they had a very definite intention to give a high literary quality to the paper and men were recruited to cover all requirements with little regard to the ability to meet the cost. Thornton Hunt was joined by George Augustus Sala (who, though always paid as a contributor, was as regular as any staff man), Edwin Arnold, a Newdigate prizeman with no newspaper experience, Edward Dicey, a scholar and lawyer, J. M. Blanchard as dramatic critic, a scholarly writer who supplemented his small earnings from the *Telegraph* by writing pantomimes, Clement Scott starting as Blanchard's assistant, Joseph Bennett as music critic,

Herbert Stack, H. B. Traill, Jeffery Prowse, only remembered perhaps for his poem ' My lost old age ' which found a place in Victorian anthologies, and many others. For many years the lighter social leaders were written by Bob Williams, a double-first at Oxford. On the news side, Le Sage and Drew Gay provided the backbone of the organization. The paper was to be more readable and the adoption of a new ' fount of type furnished by the well-known Caslon foundry ' was announced.

In the early stages of this accumulation of talent the frugal mind of J. M. Levy and the untried spirit of his son must have been sorely tested. Anxious they might be, but *audace et toujours de l'audace* was their motto. In March, 1858, an eight-page paper for one penny was produced, ' a double sheet of the size of *The Times* at fourpence '. This step was in accord with the principle that the essence of competition is to react promptly and violently, and it was the *Telegraph's* answer to the *Standard's* reduction of the price of its eight-page paper to twopence. Those who are not prepared for hard-hitting competition had better keep out of the newspaper business, and whatever the state of the income and expenditure account there was never hesitation about what to do.

Boldness was rewarded and relief was soon to come, for in 1860 expenses were reduced by £12,000 a year by the abolition of the Paper Duty, the last of the so-called taxes on knowledge. The *Telegraph* had campaigned violently for abolition, and its proprietor, with Sala, had headed a deputation to Lord Derby, the Prime Minister, who in Sala's words looked on them as Jupiter Hostis might be expected to look on an assembly of black beetles. After a struggle with the House of Lords and a general election Gladstone dispensed with the duty in his next year's budget.

The days of struggle were left behind and there was opportunity for expansion. The first necessary expansion was in accommodation. The growing newspaper had no room, and 135 Fleet Street and the buildings behind, which covered the old Peterborough Court, were purchased in 1860. The young lions had found their den.

CHAPTER II

YOUTH AND 'TRUTH'

O N October 3rd, 1861, the first untaxed *Daily Telegraph* appeared and the years of prosperity began. On December 18th, 1861, a notice appeared that the accounts had been examined by auditors who certified the sale at 141,662 copies, and in a year's time the *Daily Telegraph* claimed a circulation nearly equal to that of all the other London morning newspapers put together.

This circulation enabled advertising rates to be put up. Books, Trades, and Auctions were raised to half a crown for the first three lines and sixpence a line afterwards, Public Companies to three shillings for three lines and ninepence a line afterwards, and Births, Marriages, and Deaths to three lines for half a crown. Servants' advertisements were only one shilling for three lines. These rates were not very high compared with modern ones, but unforeseen liabilities were also lower. Twenty-five pounds was all that the *Telegraph* had to pay for libelling the soup dispensed by the refreshment room at Peterborough Station. But it was sufficient for them to learn their lesson and a leader says ' we cannot possibly stand a separate trial for every effort we make to protect the appetite and palate of our readers. Henceforward for us, all the purées and consommés of the stall where our reporters lunched at the price of £25 and costs are perfect.'

In recent years the *Daily Telegraph* supplements on great events have been a great attraction and a deserved success. The practice of their publication started early in our history and the effect on circulation was as gratifying then as now. In May, 1861, there was a four-page supplement on the International Exhibition and in March, 1863, another four-page supplement entitled 'History of the Arrival of Princess Alexandra' increased the sale of that day to 205,884 copies.

Increased revenue from sales and advertising brought an improvement in the news service. A Roving Special Correspondent in the United States covered the Civil War and supplemented the work of the regular correspondent in New York. A 'Special' covered the campaign in the South of Italy and secured an interview with Garibaldi himself. Another 'Special' followed the Maori war in New Zealand.

A survey of the principal events in the news columns of the ten years preceding the Franco-Prussian War involves us in giving the history of the times in which the *Daily Telegraph* grew to greatness, which it is the purpose of this record to avoid, and it is worth while turning from the news to the columns of opinion and having a look at what sort of guidance the young newspaper gave to its readers.

Young newspapers are not unlike young men. They start out with advanced views, hitting out wildly against established customs, but in their middle and old age they acquire greater tolerance, maybe because they have become more comfortable, possibly because they have become wiser. The young *Telegraph* crusaded against capital and corporal punishment, formed an aversion to bishops who were accused of misuse of Church revenues, and an enthusiasm for such radical proposals as life peerages. It was a young man's paper with all the exuberance of youth. Years later

Edward Lawson, when he was entertaining the Prince of Wales at Hall Barn, would have been surprised more than anything else to be reminded that his young men had accused the Prince's father of being 'no admirer of the British Constitution' and of being responsible for economies 'rather befitting a petty German Court than that of a British Sovereign'. He might have been a little shocked to find that they had attacked the Royal Family for 'seeking pensions *in forma pauperis* for their daughters whom it should be their pride and pleasure to support'. Queen Victoria had a long memory for these matters, but she was considerably mollified by the *Telegraph* leader on the death of the Prince Consort and in time was prepared to accept her son's friend as the leader of a responsible newspaper of which she became a regular reader.

The *Telegraph* was lavish with its prejudices and did not pull any punches in their expression. Tennyson had to endure a formidable broadside. He is accused of facility and affectation, and 'Idylls of the King' are a pot-boiler 'jingling without music, obsolete and not antique in diction . . . sham mediaeval panoply'. The editorial 'we', which might or might not have been Edwin Arnold, advised the Poet Laureate 'that he should produce something better for the public money. Let it be hot, Mr. Tennyson, or not at all.' I wonder what Tennyson thought of 'The Light of Asia'.

In art, the Pre-Raphaelites were accused of 'more deliberately mechanical affectation of purpose than ever'. Modernism could be accepted with limitations. 'If Mr. Whistler would leave off using muck and clay on his palette, and paint clear, like a gentleman, we should be happy to bestow any amount of praise on him, for he has all the elements of a great artist in his composition.' But gentlemanliness in art was apparently not enough. 'The Exhibition of the Royal Academy this year ought to be called the exhibition of the complete unfitness of the Royal Academy to be implicitly trusted any longer with the reputations and labours of artists.' *Plus ça change. . . .*

All young newspapers love crusades. ' The social evil' was a constant target and the *Daily Telegraph*, like hundreds of newspapers before and since, claimed to be 'the first to treat the subject of prostitution boldly and plainly'. From wherever they may have sought their meat the young lions roared loudly.

But all the booming criticism of this and that was as the twittering of a little bird compared with their abuse of the Tractarian movement. ' The little finicking man-milliners who duck and bob before crucifixes' was only warming up for the real thunder. ' Every verminous libertine who can creep into the establishment will mentally manipulate his parishioners until the prying sensuality of the Confessional, gorged with the pro-miscuous unbosomings of vice, will overflow like an inundation of disease upon society.'

It appeared to be the view of the Royal Commission on the Press that control of newspapers by editors rather than by proprietors makes for greater freedom of opinion. It may also lead to greater licence, for proprietors, who have wider considerations than personal prejudice, are more inclined to moderation. Certainly the editorial columns of the *Daily Telegraph* at this time show more evidence of the mind of Thornton Hunt or his leader writers than of its proprietors who were still fumbling for editorial direction. Edward Lawson was never a violent man and the later leaders which he inspired and amended, however definite their viewpoint, were always free from extravagant expression.

Persistently the *Telegraph* pursued its campaign for the reform of the House of Lords—' the chartered lords of misrule ogling in the ancient face of bigotry '. In other political directions it is less sure. Disraeli is far from having won his way to its heart. Of a speech at Slough ' all that glittering drapery of language has been blown to tatters and the lay figure is before us more unadorned than Dermot Macmurrough, King of Ireland, when he bathed in the blood of a white cow '. Anonymous, but the galley proof must have borne the fingerprints of Thornton Hunt.

Gladstone is hardly less unpopular, ' the voluble casuist ', ' of Jesuitical cunning ', ' so amiable and so little to be trusted ', ' we must comfort ourselves that he is not a Cabinet Minister '. Everyone was out of step except our Joseph, who felt sufficiently entrenched to accuse *The Times* of ' unscrupulous scurrility ' and ' unmitigated and unadulterated malice '.

Slowly but surely the *Telegraph* changed from its radical beginnings to a steady conservatism. The proprietors were not politically minded and were new to public affairs and in the early years the proprietorial watch-dog was wagged by the leader-writer tail. But as the proprietors got more firmly in the saddle their natural conservatism began to influence the paper. Some of the change of policy sprang from the waning of Thornton Hunt and the waxing of Edwin Arnold, and events themselves were moving very fast.

If the *Telegraph* showed inconsistency in its estimate of Disraeli was it not a fault that it shared with every man in England, not entirely excluding Disraeli himself? It is certainly a change from ' The man of disgraceful jibes and sneering sophisms ' who ' trundled to Paris and fawned upon the Emperor ', 'the Disraelian windbag of surfeited acrimony and undigested platitude ' to ' unrivalled polemical gifts of rhetoric, sarcasm, invective, ornament and governed passion '. But the change covered some twenty-five years of the most rapidly changing period of our whole history. Throughout, the

Telegraph was interpreting the changing views of its public.

There is a wide field for speculation on what is the proper function of a daily newspaper in matters of opinion. The same critics who attack the newspapers for lack of leadership inveigh against the hubristic assertion of the editorial 'we'. Who, they ask, are these few men who control newspapers and what is their qualification to tell us what we should do? The answer is that these men, just the same as any Member of Parliament, have constituents whom it is their duty to represent to the best of their ability. If the voter does not approve the views of his representative he can vote the other way, and if the reader does not like the views of his newspaper he can change his order with his newsagent. There is no lowering of purpose in the newspaper proprietor, and indeed much to commend, if he conceives it his duty to make people think, and to guide rather than to create opinion.

All these people who talk about following the crowd and failure to see the higher duty do not realize that, even if their criticism is well founded, in all judgments of merit in a newspaper the point is unimportant. Views do not rank first for the simple reason that they are views, and what really matters is the completeness, trustworthiness, and proper presentation of the news. One of Lord Camrose's first double crown posters was ' THE REAL NEWS '.

His earliest predecessors were just as mindful of its importance. Their first steps were to widen the field at home and abroad and to get as much as possible from their own correspondents. Not only the scope, but the method of news collection and the manner of its presentation were changed. Old-fashioned people who were disinterested, as well as old-fashioned newspapers which were not, had much the same hard words for the *Telegraph* as their successors had for the *Daily Mail* thirty-five years later. They accepted that it was lively and arresting, but found it vulgar and crude.

Occasionally they found it inaccurate, but not more often than is inevitable for any newspaper that rates high the time factor in the value of news. Every inaccuracy was pounced on by its competitors, especially *The Times*, and in those days the supposed doctrine in to-day's newspaper offices that dog does not eat dog was not so prevalent. Occasionally the *Telegraph* had a come-back. In December, 1864, it printed an apocryphal and rather scandalous story of an ill-tempered Turkish Princess. On the day of the apology and correction in the *Telegraph* all the other papers, including *The Times*, printed the story without verification or acknowledgment, and the following day the *Telegraph* was able to rebuke the Thunderer: ' We do not blame good old-fashioned newspapers for not having foreign correspondents of their own; the best thing that an antiquated journal can possibly do is to borrow—but to borrow with discretion.' One up, but plenty to play. The sniping continued: *The Times* conducted a campaign for cheap tea, the *Telegraph* weighed in with ' When the working men and peasants of England become universal tea-drinkers we may expect a generation of gossiping, pottering, vapid, inane and lie-abed mechanics and labourers.' The ghost of the man who wrote that must be having a most unhappy haunting of Peterborough Court, particularly if he frequents the editorial and clerical departments.

Even whilst many of the news stories were, at least compared with rival newspapers, on the light side, the feature articles were not entirely what one would expect in a ' popular ' newspaper. Many were technical and scientific such as ' The Velocity of Light ', ' Spontaneous Generation ', and a series on a new type of armaments.

'Popular' is perhaps rightly put in quotes as the proprietors had realized the growing thirst for knowledge, and this type of article was in fact attractive. Not that they were entirely influenced by the purely popular aspect of special articles. Very considerable space was given to the Volunteer movement, which was more a cause worthy of support than a reader attraction. Here again the *Daily Telegraph* has been consistent and it was in accord with tradition that it became the warmest newspaper friend of the Territorial Army.

The news net was all embracing. The *Daily Telegraph* and crime is elsewhere considered in this record. At this stage of its career it was itself conscious of treating unpleasant cases more fully than other journals critical of *Daily Telegraph* practice, 'which the public will neither buy, borrow, read nor listen to, by whom the *Daily Telegraph* is accused of dilating on the vices of the aristocracy', but it was rather the novelty of *Daily Telegraph* practice in these matters which appalled the critics than any essential turpitude. Most of the cases of which complaint was made would be reported in modern newspapers, and not only in those that specialize in the seamy side of daily happenings. But in those days of four-page papers these reports, with unusual if typographically restrained headlines, stood out like naughty deeds in a good (or hypocritical) world.

But soon in news as in views the paper began to mellow and the *Daily Telegraph* in news values set itself the high standard of responsibility which it has maintained for a century.

Perhaps at this stage, and before we consider some of the men who made the *Telegraph*, it might be profitable to break the strict chronological sequence and consider the curious episode of Labouchere and the *Telegraph*. In itself, however much interest and excitement it may have aroused at the time, it has little importance.

Labouchere was not a reliable and unbiased judge of any event, issue, institution, or individual, but when all allowance has been made for prejudice and overstatement he throws a valuable light on the *Telegraph* in its first twenty-five years.

The story is interesting and perhaps salutary for a *Daily Telegraph* historian, in the same way as it is good for any man who fancies his appearance to take a look at himself in a distorting mirror. At least he will see his blemishes clearly and if he comes away reasonably well satisfied his features probably have some merit.

During Disraeli's second administration the *Daily Telegraph* ' crossed the floor ' and became a Conservative newspaper. All the traditions of the *Daily Telegraph* were Liberal. From the beginning it supported Palmerston. For Gladstone it coined the title of ' the People's William ' and for many years Edward Lawson saw Gladstone or Montagu Corry, his confidential secretary, almost daily. The drift at first was almost imperceptible. The proprietors were beginning to be interested and amused by Disraeli and wearied by Gladstone; 'we refuse to be bored to death by philosophical radicals ', an opinion which they shared with the House of Commons. That in itself was altogether insufficient to cause a change of heart had not a growing and serious appreciation of Disraeli been fortified in the office by the counsel of Edwin Arnold who in Eastern policy was continually and vehemently against Gladstone. The break was gradual and in November, 1875, Gladstone wrote to Lawson from Chichester: ' I fear you and I are diverging rather widely—according to the present imperfect information—on a great matter recently brought into the public view; but you have probably at least the advantage of having 999 of every thousand on your side.'

One Sunday in 1876, Gladstone, after attending divine service at the Temple Church, crossed Fleet Street to the

Daily Telegraph offices. There he met Edward Lawson
and Le Sage. Gladstone said afterwards that he was
received without the least discourtesy but he saw ' there
was a firmly set purpose in their minds '. Lawson
complained, as did Queen Victoria, that Gladstone
addressed them as a public meeting.

One result of this was a violent campaign against the
Telegraph and its proprietors carried on by Henry
Labouchere in the columns of *Truth*, distinguished by the
crudest anti-Semitism and every possible accusation
against the good faith of the paper and the veracity of
its news.

Gladstone was losing many of his adherents and
J. K. Stephen wrote, though somewhat later:

> I am parted at last from the leader
> Whom I loved in the days of my youth
> Is he or am I the seceder
> T'were hard to determine the truth
> Yet my enmity is not impassioned
> I'll forgive and forget if I can.

Either the *Telegraph* or Gladstone may have been the
seceder but Labouchere's enmity against the *Telegraph*
was nothing if not impassioned. He could not forgive
nor forget. He could allow no honourable motive for
the change.

> The dissolution came
> The People's William lost his power and fame;
> The ' fetish ' that through good and bad report
> Had been the god of Peterborough Court
> Was shattered, and oh, how could he forget
> He did not first make me a baronet.
> Ungrateful Ewart! it was all for naught
> The *Telegraph* thy virtues daily taught.

And in a prose passage:

Every renegade organ of public opinion that can be
bribed into supporting the Premier, not perhaps with

money but the equivalent of money, denounces all as traitors who venture to differ from it as to the best mode to maintain the integrity of our Empire.

The equivalent of money was suggested to be the promise of information from Conservative ministers.

The only reasoned attack supported by evidence was against Drew Gay, the *Telegraph* correspondent in Constantinople, who was accused of gross inaccuracies. Drew Gay was at all times more distinguished for his enterprise than his accuracy, but Labouchere, like some modern journalist critics of the popular Press, made the mistake here and at other times of attributing every error of over-enthusiasm in the working journalist to some constructive malevolence in his proprietor.

Whatever substance there may have been in the accusations, it is obvious that in some cases Gay's authority was Mr. Layard, the British Ambassador, and in others, Turkish official sources. But neither Layard nor any Turk could ever do right for Labouchere and Gay's offence was all the ranker.

Most of the rest of the material was ridicule and vulgar abuse of the proprietors personally. J. M. Levy was allowed to be ' a good natured old man, not very refined, ignorant of politics '. The venom was reserved for his son, the editorial brains of the paper, who was personally reviled for becoming a Christian when he married out of the faith, and compared to Judas for his betrayal of Gladstone; nothing was too bad to say of him.

The campaign had two results. In an action in the Courts a jury was unable to agree on the issue of libel. If the case had been fought to-day Edward Lawson would have got a very large sum, but in those days a very different view was taken of ' fair comment ', particularly when two organs of public opinion were concerned. It was thought, and probably rightly, that those who

Thornton Hunt

Sir Edwin Arnold

Harry, Lord Burnham

Sir J. M. Le Sage

Arthur Watson

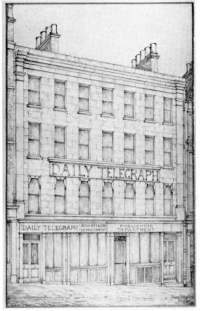

The offices of the
Daily Telegraph

1860

1882

give hard knocks must be prepared to take them. Certainly no damage was done, for the *Daily Telegraph* circulation continued to swell and its proprietors to prosper and grow in public esteem.

The second result was a bout of fisticuffs, the shortest on record until Carpentier beat Beckett, between Labouchere and Lawson outside the Beefsteak Club. The fight was less decisive than the one at the Holborn Stadium. The combatants were quickly separated, without great reluctance on either side, and both were temporarily expelled from the Club.

But the interest for the historian in the material published by *Truth* is not in the cause and course of a somewhat sordid squabble but in the light it shows on how much nearer to modern newspaper practice the *Daily Telegraph* was than any of its contemporaries.

Behind Labouchere's violent political and personal prejudice was a sincere dislike and distrust of the new journalism. Ministers should never see editors, except possibly the Editor of *The Times*, and him very occasionally. Look at what was happening!

When Mr. Gladstone was in power, up Mr. Gladstone's back stairs sneaked Ted Pry. When Lord Derby was at the Foreign Office, the same 'Ted' came creeping up Lord Derby's back stair. Since Lord Beaconsfield has been in the ascendant, the back stairs of the Premier's secretary are worn with the feet of Ted Pry.

Ted Pry is of course Edward Lawson, Editor of the paper. Political and diplomatic correspondents were then unknown and Lawson as an enterprising editor was legitimately and properly seeking information for his paper from high official sources, irrespective of who was in power.

Algernon Turnor, one of the most respected and honourable country gentlemen who ever graced

c 23

Westminster is one of the villains of the piece, 'a deputy mop squeezer of the Premier', because he maintained contacts between the Prime Minister and the *Telegraph* and other papers. He was perhaps the first P.R.O. for Downing Street.

Labouchere presumably recognized the propriety of journalists in the Press Gallery, inoffensively engaged with their shorthand reporting, but journalists in the lobby were a very different matter.

'His son is the Editor. He may be seen every day in the lobby of the House of Commons during the session button-holing members, and when he is not thus occupied he is sneaking up official back stairs to pick up scraps of news.' What a monstrous thing that the *Daily Telegraph* should have a lobby correspondent out news-getting!

The parliamentary view was different. Lawson shared alone with members of 'the faithful Commons' and Delane of *The Times* the privilege of standing at the bar of the House of Lords during debates.

The *Telegraph* Vienna correspondent, Beatty Kingston, reported what took place at a meeting between Count Andrassy and General Ignatieff. The accuracy of the account was not questioned, but this was considered highly improper because Kingston was not present at the discussion. The *Daily Telegraph* was becoming annoyingly well informed.

There are alas! a vast class of Englishmen who are fond of a journal in proportion to the airs which it assumes of being on intimate terms with great men. Look at the correspondents of the D.T.

'I am enabled on undoubted authority to state.' 'I am in a position to inform.' 'I learn from a private but official source.' 'The Government thinks.' All this sort of inventive trash, although disgusting to persons of good taste, has its effect with the millions.

But it was not inventive trash. However disgusting it might be to persons of old-fashioned taste, politicians and diplomats were beginning to talk to enterprising newspapermen in confidence that they would not be directly quoted. Kingston himself had long private interviews with Bismarck of which he could not quote a word.

Those who served the Press in the Second World War will remember that the censor gave out a list of attributions, slightly less clumsy but very similar to these, which might be used for information given by political and military leaders in off-the-record conferences.

The *Telegraph* was early to appreciate the true importance of an efficient system of communications in the equipment of a modern newspaper. They had a private wire to Paris about which Labouchere had to say this: ' I doubt whether the cause of truth is served by a newspaper having a " special wire " to some particular locality. The correspondent feels every day that he has to telegraph something, because it has already been paid for.'

The *Telegraph* was forceful in its promotion of the paper, an activity which would not appear in these days particularly indecent.

> How do ' we ' come in daily contact with public opinion? Is it by inditing articles full of senile adulation of the powers that be? Is it by cadging for advertisements? Is it by furnishing copies of the *Daily Telegraph* to the trade on sale or return?

For many years the profession of an advertisement canvasser has been considered an honourable one, and until the newsprint shortage of the Second World War ' sale or return ' was common practice in newspaper distribution.

Labouchere could not understand, or if he could understand, could not stomach that the *Daily Telegraph* was for a wide and entirely new public who had seldom or never read newspapers before, and therefore its technique, which to-day we should think sadly slow and old-fashioned, was different. 'When persons entirely unconnected with literature themselves are the owners of newspapers, they naturally sacrifice all decorum to the desire to make the journal a remunerative speculation.' The issues of a Liverpool election were 'as much beyond Lawson's ken as they are beyond that of a vendor of fried fish in Petticoat Lane'.

Lawson was indeed unconnected with literature, he was not one of the old guard of the political clubs, qualified as such to express opinions on electoral campaigns. He was a newspaperman first, last, and all the time. He employed literary men of the highest talent, none perhaps more distinguished than Edwin Arnold, but Arnold was 'a hired fanatic, who has at least the merit of believing in the snarling trash that he writes'.

The fault of the *Daily Telegraph* was that it set out to be a popular newspaper, and then as now there were men of supposed democratic views who held that for daily reading matter working men and women should have only what their betters thought was good for them. Labouchere had much of that peculiar intolerance which paradoxically is sometimes found in the purest Liberals. He could not understand this new public who wanted newspapers for the first time and newspapers of a kind different from the stodgy inhibited journals of the mid-nineteenth century. The *Daily Telegraph* was not a newspaper owned by country gentlemen and circulating to the upper classes and the intelligentsia, and so in Labby's view it was 'for the pot-house and the kitchen'. That its leading articles were written by brilliant scholars must have seemed strangely incompatible with the human-interest angle in news which Labby found such an intolerable innovation.

Of course the *Daily Telegraph* made plenty of mistakes. Mistakes will always be made by young enthusiastic men with new ideas. They were hoaxed in a man-and-dog fight story of James Greenwood's (' One of the Crowd ' and ' The Amateur Casual ') which provided their critics with good ammunition. A close check of the paper's columns would probably reveal inaccuracies but not more than are inevitable in any enterprising newspaper at any time. The speed of newspaper production makes complete accuracy impossible and the *Daily Telegraph*, unlike some of its competitors, was not waiting twenty-four hours for the publication of its news. And it was increasingly popular and successful, which particularly maddened Labby who could never forgive it the heinous crime of deserting Gladstone for Disraeli.

More and more people looked to it for news and trusted it. In a very few years it was able to carry every day the statement—

> Largest circulation in the world. The sales of the *Daily Telegraph* amount to an average which, if tested, will show an excess of half a million copies weekly over any other morning paper.

The *Daily Telegraph* had just passed its twenty-first birthday and it had come to stay.

A curious sequel to Labouchere's persistent enmity to the *Daily Telegraph* was that when Richard Pigott, the author of the Parnell forged letter, went to his house in Grosvenor Gardens to make a full confession, Labouchere called in as a witness George Augustus Sala, a neighbour and still on the staff of the *Telegraph*. The document was initialled by Pigott on every page and signed by Labby and Sala, and so the paper which Labby hated was given an incomparable story.

Labouchere always kept the bitterness in his heart, or

wherever one keeps bitterness, but Gladstone himself cherished no animosities and chose the *Daily Telegraph* for the publication of his last literary work, three long columns of 'Personal Recollections of Arthur H. Hallam'. On his death four months later rules were turned in mourning, a rare tribute to a private citizen.

CHAPTER III

VIXERE FORTES

AMONG the great men of the *Daily Telegraph* the
strangest, and in some ways the greatest, was
George Augustus Sala (*D.T.* 1857–93). Adjectives to
describe him are difficult to find. Flamboyant, exotic,
egoistic, bombastic, unconventional, eccentric,
omniscient, all would fit and there are plenty more.

His first entry into the office gave promise of a
picturesque career. Years later at Brighton Sir Edward
Lawson described it in Sala's presence. The young
recruit, only twenty-nine years old, wore a chocolate
coloured frock coat, a double-breasted plaid velvet
waistcoat, trousers of uncertain colour and much too
short, and blucher boots. Sala only disagreed with the
description of the waistcoat which he maintained was
black camlet profusely embroidered with beads and
bugles of jet. Later he always wore the white waistcoat
which appears in the cartoon. Later too his nose, that
gift to caricaturists, was broken. Many stories are
told of the circumstances of this happening but no one
can dispute the verdict of the *Daily Telegraph* printer who
said, 'If only Mr. Sala had been at home writing his
copy this would never have happened.'

The choice of Sala was not as much a gamble as some
of the proprietors' selections of young men. His
training and experience were extensive and peculiar—
scene painter, playwright, librettist, lithographer, etcher,

29

copyist of legal documents, and novelist, all at twenty-nine years of age. In some of these arts he excelled and he was commissioned by Ackerman to etch on a series of large plates a panorama view of the funeral procession of the Great Duke. His novel writing was perhaps the least recommendation, as he had just published *The Baddington Peerage* which he himself described at the time as the worst novel ever perpetrated, a judgment which he confirmed thirty years later. He had a much better qualification in that he had made some reputation as a writer of notes and essays in *Household Words*, then edited by Charles Dickens.

Actually Sala was always paid as a contributor and was never on the salary list of the *Telegraph*, though for all practical purposes he might as well have been as he always held himself entirely at its disposal.

To supplement his earnings which were never adequate for his expenditure he preferred to be allowed to contribute to other journals, which he did freely. Some cannot have been very remunerative. 'Damn the *Entertainment Gazette*,' said Sala. 'They owe me three weeks' salary and now they want to sell me the paper.'

Sala's versatility was tremendous. In 1881 he received a message, 'Please write a leader on Billingsgate and the price of fish, and start for St. Petersburgh this evening.' That message gives a fair suggestion of the range within which he wrote easily, forcefully, amusingly and with a vast fund of curious knowledge. In forty years' service he wrote fewer than forty articles on political subjects. As he wrote in his life story, ' The idea of the proprietors was that it should be not only a thoroughly comprehensive newspaper, but also a miscellany of human and descriptive social essays, and in these respects a kind of daily *Household Words* . . . and what they yearned for was a staff of writers, who possessed, first of all a lively style, and who next, had seen something of the world, both in London and Paris and who finally could turn out plenty of copy.' He concluded this passage with the observation that he was their man, and undoubtedly he was.

His energy matched his versatility. He records that in one period of twenty-four hours he wrote two leaders, attended the Private View of the Royal Academy and wrote a notice, saw and described the ' Talking Fish ' which was being exhibited at the Egyptian Hall, and finally attended the annual dinner of the Royal Literary Fund and a charity ball at Willis's Rooms, writing an account of both events. On such matters, and indeed on every subject and on news events of all kinds, volunteers shooting at Wimbledon, or Orsini shooting at Napoleon III, as ' The Siliad ' has it—

> Salaneus through the Kosmos rove
> To aid us with encyclopaedic lore,
> To write as poets never wrote before;
> Too superfine, our native tongue to use
> Unless adorned with epithets profuse;
> And our High Muse instruct the chiefs to lot
> In bastard Green or limping Polyglot.

Sala treated criticism of his style and methods with genial resentment :

Let the Special be a crass donkey, or a blockhead, or a mere respectable mediocrity, and his letters will pass without much comment. . . . But let the Special only be so unfortunate as to have a style of his own—let him have a capacity for minute observation, or a gift for picturesque and vivid description; let him be endowed with the power of thinking, and of expressing his thoughts in vivid language —and the whole of Hampstead Heath will be upon him at once . . . to accuse him, if he happens to mention that he has dined with a duke or conversed with a general, of being a flunkey, a toady, a Jenkins and a lickspittle; to insinuate, if he happens to advance the claims of this or

31

that political party, of being bribed by them; and in particular, when he is doing his best to tell the truth, to brand him as an impudent and deliberate liar; these are the amenities to which every Special Correspondent who has attained eminence in his vocation must look forward as his continuous and inevitable portion.

He cannot have been so sensitive to criticism of his eccentricities of style, for he was allowed by Burnand to parody his own ' Echoes of the Week ' in *Punch* and very savagely and amusingly he did it.

Criticism of his eccentricities of behaviour he took more hardly, possibly because he was more vulnerable, and indeed he was tested highly.

> If the Genius gets in the hands of the Jews, is often drunk, always in debt, sometimes in prison, and is totally dis-reputable, living *à tort et à travers* the rules of society, these newspaper proprietors think more and more of him, and go down on their knees and bribe him to write.

Certainly he had never been in prison, and the rest, if with a faint suspicion of truth, was sufficiently libellous to cause this passage and more like it to cost Haine Friswell £500 in the courts. What would it have cost him to-day?

It is quite clear that Sala, with all his oddities of style, dress, and behaviour, can never have been the dis-reputable figure painted by Friswell and his enemies. He enjoyed the friendship of men of eminence in many walks of life, in a highly decorous and intolerant age he was not only received but was on close personal terms with many society hostesses, he stayed with Lord Rose-bery at Mentmore, and though Lord Rosebery was more concerned with intelligence in his guests than social standing or behaviour he would never have entertained the disreputable scallywag of Old Frizzle's *Modern Men of Letters*.

One can give a caricature or a picture of the man, one can record his travels, give long lists of the subjects of his articles, but even by printing copious extracts from them one can convey little idea of his contribution to the success of the *Telegraph*. It is necessary to understand the new public, wanting not only news from a wider field written in a more lively way and more attractively presented, but also what we should now call magazine and feature material which the *Daily Telegraph* was first to provide. Sala brilliantly supplied all these needs.

In any quiz to-day how many intelligent, reasonably well educated people under fifty could answer what the name of George Augustus Sala suggests? A few might say ' Bohemian ', ' Telegraphese ', or even ' young lion ', but of these how many would know much more?

What do we remember of any except the most eminent Victorians? Sala's friend Alexis Soyer, the Macaulay *de l'art culinaire*, for whom Sala wrote the *catalogue raisonné* of Soyer's Symposium restaurant at Gore House, has left a name, but only as the deviser of a particularly utilitarian form of army stove, and I doubt if any soldier of either World War who benefited by his invention knew anything about the celebrated cook, restaurateur, and social figure of the eighteen-fifties.

It is not surprising that we should forget these glittering personalities. Who remembers a picture that is a mass of confused colour, however brilliant? The poet, the dramatist, or even the novelist may achieve long life, or near immortality—the journalist writes only for his day and hardly lives beyond it.

Sala's best newspaper work was particularly of his day, for it lay not in the social and literary comment, essays on every conceivable subject from ' The Hats of Humanity ' to ' The Art of William Hogarth ', so much as in his dispatches as Special Commissioner, as he called himself, in Russia, in America, in the Civil War, in

Italy in the War of Liberation, in France in 1870, in Spain, in Greece and at many other times and in many other places in this country and all over Europe. He was never, in the strict sense, a war correspondent and the military side of his wartime assignments was covered by others, but wherever there was anything big enough in war or peace, at home or abroad, the *Telegraph* sent Sala. He knew well what his proprietors wanted and his instructions from them were simple and short. ' GO ODESSA SEE MOB GO CONSTANTINOPLE' was the simple six word message he got at Warsaw in 1876. Sala knew that he was to cover the Russian mobilization and then follow the war, if it broke out, from the Turkish side, and without query or further brief Sala went.

However popular his other work at the time, critical opinion varies about its real worth, but no one can dispute that he was a great reporter. Contemporary estimates of Sala vary according to the height of the brow or perhaps the depth of the spleen. Sir Sydney Lee says:

> The facility with which he drew upon his varied stores of half-digested knowledge, the self-confidence with which he approached every manner of topic, the egoism and the bombastic circumlocutions which rapid production encouraged in him, hit the taste of a large section of the public.

W. B. Maxwell, the novelist, writes:

> He won renown and praise all over the English-speaking world for his erudite and yet humorous articles and essays. His knowledge of out-of-the-way subjects was colossal, and he wove his queer lore into a sort of running commentary on London life. It was generally said that rare thought, graceful comment, sheer art, made a fountain of delight that bubbled continuously from Sala's page.

The truth was probably somewhere between the two

What mattered to the *Daily Telegraph* was that Sala hit the taste of a large section of the public, nor could anybody accuse him of writing down to them.

Near the end he was very ill in Paris and a member of the staff called on behalf of the proprietors to inquire about his health. The sick man, perhaps faintly recalling an earlier message about fish, sat up in bed and said, ' Tell them I am ready to write about anything from the price of beef to a Coronation.' He did not live eight years to write about a Coronation. That privilege went to a man about as different from Sala as two men could be—J. L. Garvin. It takes all sorts to make a *Telegraph*. Sala's last assignment was not a Coronation but the wedding of a future King of England, George, Duke of York. As a *Telegraph* man and a low-brow, if I have to spend an evening with a ghost in Fleet Street, I would as soon meet George Augustus Sala as Samuel Johnson.

Putting Sala in the lead of this chapter is not a verdict of ' Eclipse First '. There is no attempt to make a handicap of the many distinguished, able, and even peculiar men who made the *Daily Telegraph* and there is no order of merit in the list of names. Perhaps Clement Scott comes next in my thought because like Sala he was so very much of a Victorian, though typical newspapermen, however eminent, vary very little in their essential qualities through the years or even in different countries.

It is impossible to compare Clement Scott (*D.T.* 1871–98) with the critics of to-day, as the style and scope of dramatic criticism have so vastly changed. Then as now there were good and bad critics. It would appear to be an occupational disease of many of even the best critics at all times to be unable to stick to their strict purpose, which is to notice the play. The divagations were then to show their immense erudition, now their devastating smartness.

Scott's notice of the Bancroft revival of *The School for Scandal* in 1874 has some three thousand seven hundred words before he ever gets down to the play at all. The first part, twelve hundred words, is historical, recalling such seemingly irrelevant matters as that at the time of the writing of the play the Earl of Chatham was on the eve of his death, Dr. Dodd was being executed for forgery, and Horne Tooke was close upon his trial for a seditious declaration.

But at least it must be said that in contrast to some modern critics, who in their restricted space can only scintillate at the expense of the play, Scott's show of erudition was supplementary and this prodigious preface includes an eleven-hundred-word analysis of the play and is followed by some fifteen hundred words of unadulterated review of the first-night performance.

Clement Scott came to the *Telegraph* from the *Observer* as assistant to Blanchard, whom he soon succeeded as first critic though Blanchard continued till 1887. First-night notices till that time were hardly heard of. Not only was the *Telegraph* breaking new ground in the practice of giving them regularly but Scott himself made something of an innovation in his method. He aimed to give ' not a solemn and serious criticism but a picturesque report '. Hitherto so-called dramatic criticism had been for the most part mere reports. ' I wanted . . . to make them attractive; to compel people to read them; to make them light and lively, and in accordance with the oncoming newspaper spirit of the age.' Scott like all members of the *Telegraph* staff was very conscious of this new spirit and that they were the pioneers of a new newspaper age.

Scott could not accept all that the newer journalism involved. He deplored that ' news about the drama is not postponed till the actors and actresses have learned their words and studied their business '.

In his theatre notices his style was more impersonal than in his descriptive writing; there are nine I's in the first eight lines of his description of Queen Victoria's Diamond Jubilee procession. But if his style avoided the first person pronoun, his views were intensely personal and emotional.

Though Scott maintained that the journalist who cannot write at top speed should not represent a daily newspaper, most of his work shows obvious evidence of the midnight oil, though it would be a mistake to come to that conclusion entirely from the length of his notices. Once he had decided his first sentence in the cab from the theatre to Fleet Street, he wrote at prodigious speed and could turn out a column of the small print then used in three-quarters of an hour.

His influence in the theatre of the day was undoubtedly very great though to modern students of his work a little difficult to understand. His depths were inconsiderable, but his judgments appealed to the great middle class of the day who formed the *Daily Telegraph* readership. His ideal was the well constructed play; he did not think that it was for the stage to deal with any serious problems and he had a predilection for the happy ending. 'The trouble is when dramatists insist upon giving pain and bringing down the gloom of mist, when sunshine might just as easily be seen.'

These limitations he shared with the critics of his day. It is perhaps unreasonable to fault a man for not being in advance of his time, and in some ways Scott broke new ground in that he made the theatre live and inspire interest in a wider public.

Probably he conscientiously believed himself to be a modern, and at least he showed it in his continual fight for greater realism in stage performance, but in all that mattered he was no sort of a modern at all. The extreme example of this was his part in the Ibsen controversy, in which he appears far from well, not so much in his dislike of the plays, which is not peculiar to him, but in the violence of his expression of it, which shows little trace of critical judgment.

Always full of personal prejudices, in writing about plays he was an impressionist and a partisan and his writing was picturesque to a fault, but nobody could dispute that he was the most interesting critic of his day nor that vast importance was attached by managers and public to his views. Those views, profound or not, coincided with the opinion of the public and Scott's authority was enhanced by the fact that he was the finest judge of acting in his time or perhaps any other.

It would not be fair to examine how far some of his enthusiastic judgments have stood the test of time. Many far more judicial critics would fare no better, but perhaps they would not stick out their necks so far.

'*Olivia* will live in the after generations as a standard English play.' Who remembers W. G. Wills' *Olivia*? Possibly Scott did not appreciate how much it owed to Ellen Terry on that first night in 1878. Scott thought that *The Notorious Mrs. Ebbsmith* was 'the best, most interesting, and most convincing of Mr. Pinero's realistic plays' and he believed that '*Sweet Lavender* will perfume the stage to-morrow when *The Second Mrs. Tanqueray* and *Gay Lord Quex* are at rest in the cemetery of dead drama:

Of his style I cannot do better than record the verdict of his more scholarly successor, W. L. Courtney :

> He wrote a marvellous style, a style which could not be ignored, so considerable was its range and so persuasive its appeal. No doubt in his hands it was effective enough, but from any literary standards its faults were obvious. Scott's prose was a very rhythmical affair; it was often on the verge of blank verse when its business was to encourage or upbraid, and when it desired to rend an opponent to

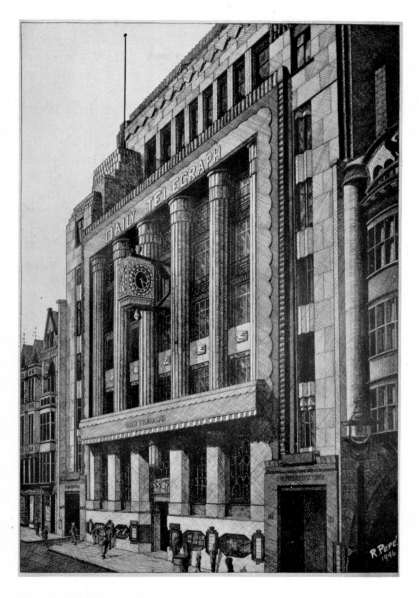

The *Daily Telegraph*, 1930. The frontage is nearly double that of the 1882 building in the illustration facing page 23

Staff delegation at Hall Barn for Edward Lord Burnham's 80th birthday

Back Row—H. Meek, E. T. Williamson, W. R. Williamson, Francis Caine, D. Ross Williams
Middle Row—C. A. Reeve, H. C. Bailey, J. B. Firth, E. C. Bentley, Fred Miller, J. Hall Richardson,
John Martin, Sidney Galtrey, W. M. Southey, Frank Hare, The Hon. Harry Lawson

pieces it became a lyrical scream. It could be pompous and rhetorical, bombastic and full of rodomontade, sentimental and sickly, with a kind of eloquence that was Scott's own.

This style with its verbiage, its ornamentation, and its overemphasis was typical of his time. What was Scott's own was a quality in the matter, manner, and method of his writings which gave him an unchallenged position above all his colleagues. We may think what we like of his style to-day, but Matthew Arnold must then have preferred it to Sala's.

The legend that Scott did not approve Irving's performance in *The Bells* and was induced by J. M. Levy to alter his notice has been corrected in Laurence Irving's life of his grandfather. Scott's admiration of the performance was intensified by J. M. Levy's enthusiasm but was entirely spontaneous.

His notorious attack on the morals of the stage did not, as has been generally thought, appear in the *Telegraph* but in an interview in a magazine called *Great Thoughts*. Scott's thoughts in the matter were as foolish as they were incomprehensible and could in no way be described as great, but the article was not nearly so sensational as those who have not read it might think. In this age of exaggeration it would have excited slight or, at most, transient interest; then, however, it raised a storm of indignation and Scott's popularity with players and managements disappeared in a morning. Irving somewhat unwillingly, but representing the profession, called on Le Sage at Peterborough Court. Surely if this had been more than a formal demonstration he would have seen his great friend Edward Lawson. But if Irving, as his grandson has recorded, kept his head, the rage of the profession was intense and Scott sent in his resignation. Edward Lawson, too, did not lose his sense of proportion and refused to accept it but insisted on Scott publishing an explanation and apology.

Scott continued his work for the *Telegraph* but not for long. The reason for his leaving in 1898 was that Edward Lawson would not agree to Scott's signing his theatre notices, a practice which was contrary to the style of the paper. Scott's great fault had always been his inordinate vanity and he threatened to resign. Edward Lawson was not a good man to threaten, and though he urged Scott to think again Scott refused, and Scott went.

Clement Scott, like Sala and others of those spacious days, has experienced debunking and rehabilitation. His eminence which was unquestionable in his day should not be diminished by time, his failings were those of all contemporary writers, and particularly of all theatrical writers. The assessor should regard not only the man and his writings but the English stage in his working life, and there is not scope in this book for a review of the Victorian theatre.

Its progress in popularity and in standards of performance in some fifty years was beyond belief and no one can dispute the importance of Scott's contribution to that progress. He came to the *Telegraph* after the early struggles were over and its circulation was a very wide one, and in his criticisms and notes he made the theatre one of the principal and most attractive interests of the newspaper. The vastly greater audience which the stage could claim in the nineties would not have come, or would have come very much later, but for Clement Scott and the *Daily Telegraph*.

Though the *Daily Telegraph* was already a popular newspaper by the time Clement Scott joined the staff, its interest and circulation were increased by his contribution. Actors and actresses, who, as now, never read their notices, snatched the *Daily Telegraph* first from the pile of newspapers brought to their breakfast tables or their bedsides on the morning after the first night. Managers made no bones about doing the same, because they knew how much the success of the venture depended on what Scott had to say, and for good reason, because at the very same moment many a worthy and substantial citizen was opening his *Daily Telegraph* and reading hurriedly through those closely packed columns to decide whether he and his wife and perhaps the older members of the family should see the play.

As his counterpart does to-day, he may have grumbled faintly that this paper and this man make too much of these people (he did not know the word 'glamourize') but as he folded his paper and went to catch his train or his omnibus he probably said, 'I know, my dear, its news may be a bit sensational but we can't afford to be without the *D.T.*'

Mention of sensationalism brings us naturally back to Drew Gay. Drew Gay was one of the early builders who was somewhat more slapdash with the bricks and mortar than many of his fellow workers on the news side.

The *Daily Telegraph*, as happens with newspapers, had amongst the solid toilers a considerable leaven of intellectuals and toughs. Drew Gay was unquestionably among the toughs. His natural talent was that of a news editor and at any time he would have been a great one. In the struggle for authority at the *Telegraph* he had always against him the steady competence of Le Sage who had much of Gay's qualities with the advantage of greater reliability and consequently more confidence from his chief. When Le Sage was on assignments at home or abroad Drew Gay had the principal hand in the news gathering organization and made the most of it.

Like many newspapermen of his type he was frequently in trouble. As special correspondent in Constantinople he was violently attacked by Labouchere, as recorded elsewhere, and he fell foul of Wolseley in

Egypt. The Constantinople incident may not have bothered him much but Egypt was a deep humiliation, for he had to be rescued by his rival, Le Sage.

As with many distinguished newspapermen his enterprise occasionally went to his head, but his contribution to the liveliness and news value of the paper was very considerable. In another chapter is related his part in the Bravo mystery, and many anonymous coups revealed in a study of the files bear the stamp of Drew Gay. More than many in this book Drew Gay is a legend and, as often happens, the memory of his misdemeanours lingers more strongly than that of his sound achievement. Much of the legend may be false but the following story is well vouched for, and is typical of the man.

Drew Gay gate-crashed into a constituency party held at the Reform Club after the Liberal defeat of 1874. To his dismay he recognized a rival who had done the same and who fortunately did not know him. Gay strode up to him and asked his constituency and got the answer ' Salford ', probably the first name that occurred to the man's mind. ' Salford? ' said Gay. ' Then you're a damned Tory, you've no business here.' The interloper fled and Gay got a column story to himself.

There seems to be no exact record of his service which was for some twenty-five years in the first forty of the paper's existence, nor can I find any description of him except as ' a military-looking fellow '. I think, if he were alive to-day, we might lose him to the *Daily Express*.

Drew Gay's alleged inaccuracies gave *Truth* its most reliable ammunition for its attack on the *Daily Telegraph*, but if Labby's target was the man chiefly responsible for the paper's change of policy on the Near East question he should have fired more shots at Edwin Arnold.

Arnold's engagement was one of the most speculative and successful of Edward Lawson's choices and gives high testimony to his judgment. Arnold (*D.T.* 1862–

1900) was a Newdigate prize winner and despite his youth had for five years been Principal of Poona College. He came home ill and answered an advertisement in the Athenaeum for an editorial writer for a London morning newspaper. On interview he had to admit that he had never been in a newspaper office before. Lawson set him to write a leading article on the Prusso-Danish crisis and engaged him on the spot. The next week he wrote six leaders, which in those more toilsome days was only part of the editorial writer's stint. Everything he wrote was distinguished by imagination, scholarship, and a fund of knowledge. To be accused by Sala of all men of ' an Oriental exuberance of epithets ' he must have thought a little unfair, though being the most courteous, amiable, and unjealous man who ever served the *Telegraph* he would never have complained of harder words than these.

I remember him as a rugged, rather ugly old man in a black velvet skull cap. This was not a habit of old age as he had worn it for many years. This, his sallow face, and the rosette of the Order of Medjidie in his button-hole made him a somewhat exotic figure in a Fleet Street office. Le Sage always said that Arnold was a Buddhist, certainly he was a fatalist in all things, with the soft serene dignity of an Oriental mystic. For all that he was capable of intense application to mundane issues and found his chief employment in the writing of political articles. No leader writer of those days was confined to leaders and Arnold did much other work. The rewrite man is considered a modern innovation but Bennett Burleigh's literary reputation owes a good deal to Arnold's presentation of his copious and vivid messages. Arnold must have realized how different was the tempo of Fleet Street from that of Oxford and Poona when the scholar and poet was set by Le Sage to produce in six hours a leader and a poem on Piper Findlater's gallantry on the heights of Dargai. Both were delivered with a few minutes to spare.

> ' Men of the Gordon Highlanders ! '
> Colonel Matthias loudly cries,
> ' The General's orders are to take
> At any needful sacrifice
> Yonder position: His we'll make it
> The Gordon Highlanders will take it.'

It was a long poem, but even considering that it was a rush job it can hardly have made Tennyson jealous though the Laureate himself was not incapable of doggerel. The leader on a meeting at Exeter Hall in connection with an engineering dispute shows more of the *labor limae* and must have taken a good share of the six hours. *Telegraph* writers certainly had to be versatile.

In all his intense activity in Peterborough Court, Arnold found time eighteen years after his entry to write his one great poem ' The Light of Asia '.

Perhaps Arnold's success emboldened the proprietors to consider the possibilities of professors in foreign universities. The recruitment of Dr. E. J. Dillon was in some ways similar to that of Arnold. The difference was that Arnold applied for a job and Dillon was persuaded to take one, and Dillon had at least written prose, however abstruse and literary.

Dillon was discovered in the early nineties by Harry Lawson when on a visit to Russia. He was employed as a professor of languages in a Russian university. The son of an Irish revolutionary father and an English mother and married to a Russian, he knew well every country in Europe except Ireland where he was born. He was, as I remember him, a greyish little man with a stubbly beard, a soft voice and a quiet manner, distinguished only by his complete lack of distinction until he started talking. Dillon claimed to speak twenty-six languages, as against Richard Burton's thirty-five, but only ten with complete fluency, and a mere five well enough to be taken for a native of the country. Certain it is that he wrote a book on the ancient Bactrian language and the Zend Avesta in French, translated the metrical portions of the Old Testament from Hebrew, and wrote articles on Armenia in German and a history of mediaeval Scandinavian literature in Russian.

As a roving foreign correspondent he somehow always contrived to arrive in a capital the day before trouble broke. His enemies said that the value of his intelligence system and his news sense were proved when without warning Cherif Pasha he cancelled his arrangement to accompany him on the Brussels carriage drive when the attempt was made on his life.

His knowledge of the Chancelleries of Europe and their occupants was extensive and peculiar. He was on close personal terms with most of the leading politicians on the continent and one of his coups was an interview on board ship with his friend Count Witte, the Russian plenipotentiary, on his way to New Hampshire to negotiate the peace treaty with Japan. Sent by wireless telegraphy, at that stage of the invention the message had to be relayed between four ships. His knowledge of the men and the issues made him an invaluable interpreter of the tangled international politics of the years before the First World War.

Dillon's greatest achievement for the *Daily Telegraph* was his Armenian mission in 1895, and his despatches on the atrocities created a sensation. Sir Philip Currie, the Ambassador, was requested by the Grand Vizier to order Dillon out of the Ottoman Empire and answered that it was beyond his powers. Sir Ashmead Bartlett in the House of Commons denied that there was any British correspondent in Armenia and questioned the authenticity of Dillon's messages. Sir Edward Grey declared that he knew the *Daily Telegraph* had a special correspondent there, but refused to give his name.

Dillon was 'underground' in Armenia, sometimes disguised as a Kurdish chief, sometimes as a Turkish woman. To his challengers he was able to produce the evidence of American missionaries who looked after him when he was ill, and he had also taken the precaution of being photographed with a Kurdish chief under sentence of death, with whom by bribing the head of the prison he was enabled to have an interview. This man's avowals formed the basis of Gladstone's historic speech at Chester, and an odd sequel to the chapter of *Daily Telegraph* history in which Labouchere in defence of Gladstone impugned the veracity of Drew Gay, the *Telegraph* correspondent in Constantinople.

Dillon had a 'cloak and dagger' complex and disguise had a fascination for him. In 1897 he succeeded in getting to Crete because the Russian Consul-General was an old school friend. Despite all restrictions he got through to the interior, lived with Venizelos and the insurgents dressed as a monk, and at Suda Bay acted as interpreter between them and the Italian and Austrian admirals who were blockading the port. All passed well until their departure, when Canevaro, the Italian Admiral, asked the monk to give him his blessing. Dillon recited the first verse of the third ode of Anacreon over his bent head and the party closed in harmony.

Dillon was generally employed on roving missions over Europe in accordance with his own suggestions. Occasionally he was specially directed to assignments considered worthy of his pen. One of the most notable of these was the second trial of Dreyfus in 1899, and day after day he sent an average of four columns. I give the closing of his story as an illustration of Dillon's style and of the manner of descriptive reporting at the end of the century.

Colonel Jouaust's voice was unsteady, and seemed to have a funereal ring in it as he held up three sheets of paper in his left hand and read out the judgment. Was his voice loud enough for Captain Dreyfus in his little room away off the hall to hear? Few people knew what he was reading. An unerring instinct kept them on the watch for the essential words. Suddenly we heard, ' Yes; the accused man is guilty ', and a shudder convulsed the frames of the public.

Thus hope mocks Dreyfus like a demon's laugh. But had we heard aright? I, for my part, could hear nothing further.

I saw naught but Colonel Jouaust's bleached head and his thick white moustache. The speaking, waxen face grew bigger and bigger, absorbing all things else in the hall, whirling round and round, framed in a ring of darkness, to the accompaniment of a sing-song sound which seemed inarticulate until the words ' extenuating circumstances ', ' ten years' seclusion ', struck my ears. Then I noted the flood of light bathing the hall, the deep calm of the blue heaven visible through the open window, and the contrast between this tranquillizing frame and the blood-curdling picture made an everlasting impression upon my soul.

Dillon outlived his value. As he grew older he became discursive and at times almost incomprehensible. Always a man of strong and sometimes violent opinions, he became less and less objective and more and more difficult to use, and towards the end of the Versailles Conference he retired to Mexico and then to Spain.

Amongst these brilliant, colourful, temperamental, and sometimes erratic characters stands out the sturdy figure of John Le Sage. The others wrote copiously in the columns of the paper and their articles are stamped with their personality, they wrote books which give clear pictures of themselves and of their methods.

John Le Sage did none of these things. Such of his work as appeared in print was straight reporting marked by the solid ability that distinguished all he did. Asked to write his reminiscences he declined because he said that the information gained by a man in his working life was not his property but that of the organization which employed him, a strange doctrine in these days when at any age from forty onwards men of very little worth rush to their publishers with their autobiographies.

It is, therefore, more difficult to judge what sort of man he was. In a tribute to him on his completion of fifty years' service with the paper Harry Lawson spoke of his sublime common sense amounting almost to genius. Le Sage knew instinctively what Edmund Yates's man on the knifeboard of the omnibus was thinking and what he wanted in his daily paper. In the early days the staff were a miscellaneous party. There was plenty of knowledge, plenty of ability, and plenty of flair, but practical experience was often varied and sometimes lacking. The Levys were printers, Thornton Hunt's practical editorial experience was a few months in each of the chairs of the *North Cheshire Reformer* and the *Argus* in Glasgow, Arnold had never been in a newspaper office, Dicey was a lawyer, Dillon a professor. Le Sage with his thorough grounding on the *Western Morning News* was the completely experienced craftsman and throughout he was the adjutant to the man known in the office as 'the young governor'. Not only in military campaigns is it difficult to assess the respective contribution to victory of the commander and the chief staff officer. Le Sage joined the *Daily Telegraph* eight years after its birth and continued, with a very short interval of ill-health, till 1923. Shortly after joining, he was placed in his own words 'on Lord Burnham's personal staff' and for the greater part of his service, whatever his title, he was the principal executive member of the editorial staff.

It is difficult to say precisely how long Le Sage was Editor of the paper. In his early years as Edward Lawson's personal assistant he was in effect News Editor of the paper, but during that time he filled many special assignments. He went to Marseilles to meet Stanley on his return from the discovery of Livingstone, and out of this meeting arose Stanley's second African adventure, the journey across the Dark Continent financed by the *Daily Telegraph* and the *New York Herald*. He was at Chislehurst for the death of the Emperor Napoleon, he 'scooped' the death of Palmerston, he interviewed Sitting Bull, he was in Egypt for the bombardment of Alexandria, and was the first to tell Lord Derby that Disraeli had ordered the British Fleet to enter the Dardanelles without the knowledge of his Foreign Minister. In exchange for this news he not unnaturally had the first information of Lord Derby's resignation.

Le Sage's last coup as a correspondent was his greatest in giving the *Telegraph* the first news of the entry of the Germans into Paris in January, 1872. *The Times* had arranged for a special train from Paris to Calais where a special boat was waiting. Le Sage got a special train to Lille where the wires were open and arranged for a special edition of the *Telegraph* at midnight.

In the getting of all news stories there is an element of luck. Le Sage and Sala were sent to represent the *Daily Telegraph* at the Coronation of the Tsar Alexander III in 1883. It was practically impossible to obtain a seat in the Cathedral for any correspondent. One ticket was finally secured for the *Telegraph* on the personal intervention of the Duke of Edinburgh.

Sala was the better writer, Le Sage the keener newsgetter, but a very different factor decided the issue of who should have the story. Both were informed before leaving London that for all important functions uniform was essential. This left Le Sage unmoved as he was a Deputy Lieutenant of the City of London. Sala's taste in dress was peculiar rather than formal, but protesting that the only court he recognized was Peterborough Court he succeeded in borrowing or hiring a suit of English Court Dress. The officials at the door of the Cathedral preferred gold and scarlet to black velvet and lace and the officer of the Guard closed the door of the carriage on Sala and ordered it away.

When he was not on these various engagements Le Sage was the mainspring of the office and when Arnold was a sick man in the later years of his Editorship, Le Sage acted for him. He did not retire till 1923 though for the last years he was staying on to complete his sixty years in Fleet Street and his work was largely done by Fred Miller who succeeded him.

Miller died from a sudden illness, having served little more than a year in full enjoyment of the Editor's chair.

Of Le Sage's share in the success of the first fifty years it is impossible to speak too highly. He was one of the few of the early days who had a thorough newspaper experience. He provided the solid backing of professional competence to a brilliant and enthusiastic staff. T. P. O'Connor, who worked with him, described him as a man ' who took everything seriously but nothing tragically, and who had the sober and realistic common sense that faced things as they came, and knew neither exultation nor despair '. ' T.P.' ended with the comment, ' It is the steady workmen like Le Sage who keep the world going.' Most men with whom I have discussed him have commented on his silence. Those who only knew him in extreme old age have even suggested that he was a Sphinx without a secret. Perhaps they appreciated insufficiently that if most of your working days have been spent with Sala, Scott, Arnold, and Dillon it was not often your turn to speak. Le Sage was silent because he had no great gift of verbal expression, but when he spoke it was to the point, clear and authoritative.

His appearance both in middle and old age was that of a rather dull and stupid man, but he was far from being either. He may have had little fire in his belly, but he certainly had a very wise head on his shoulders. There was no call for any flow of words in the office. Under his master he kept plenty of dogs and had no need to bark himself.

The bright occasional stars could attract the expanding reading public to the new paper. Le Sage knew that whatever may attract a man to a newspaper there is only one thing that will keep him as a reader day in and day out, that is that the newspaper should keep him well informed. Le Sage saw that the columns of the *Daily Telegraph* were filled with news, comprehensive, accurate, and up to date. In those days of improving but still scanty communications there was a full field for the organizing talent of the newsman and Le Sage filled it with unfaltering energy, devotion, and skill. In Edward Lord Burnham's last message to Le Sage he said, ' God bless you, old friend; whatever happens now, we have had a great time together, we have done big things in a big way.'

CHAPTER IV

FOREIGN CORRESPONDENTS

OF the *Daily Telegraph* resident foreign correspondents in the nineteenth century the most
remarkable was William Beatty Kingston. The elder
Goodman who had to handle the work of all the leading
members of the editorial staff for some fifty odd years
recorded his view that Kingston was ' the most brilliant
man the *Telegraph* ever had in its service '. Kingston's
standing was high both in Prussia, the country of his
accreditation, and in Peterborough Court. Although
for a time more formal, he was soon addressing the
younger proprietor as ' Dear Edward ' in letters closely
packed with background information.

His headquarters were Berlin, but he spent much
of his time in Vienna and had a roving commission as
Central European Correspondent.

Bismarck had considerable respect for him despite the
suspicion, common to all autocratic régimes, of correspondents who speak the language well enough to be
taken for a native—and, in fact, it is fairly evident that
Bismark cordially disliked him. Kingston was a vast
man of inordinate vanity and a very independent mind.
' An old diplomat ' in a magazine article described him
thus:

> The fact was that B. K. who stood 6 ft. 4 ins. in his stock-
> ings, stalwart and burly in proportion, bearded like a pard,
> high-coloured, with a voice and a laugh of the most sonorous

52

character, his hat rakishly perched on one side of his head and with a perfectly inimitable cavalry swagger, was entirely devoid of the bump of reverence. . . . His effrontery with the great of the earth was colossal, of a nature to paralyse old-fashioned courtiers. It pleased the Anointed of the Lord and the great of the earth to meet a man without a trace of the obsequiousness that characterized the majority of those by whom they were approached.

It may usually have done so, but it did not please the Iron Chancellor who probably found that his physical and mental dominance fell short of what he was accustomed to enjoy in his dealings with newspapermen.

Nevertheless, in a conversation of some hours in September, 1867, what Kingston, in his letter of report, calls ' The Man ' began, ' I have experience of your discretion—I shall therefore have no concealment from you—but I reckon confidently upon your using all the personal part of what I may tell you with all necessary reserve—and you will understand that the more unreservedly I speak to you, the greater proof I give you of my conviction that you will not compromise me with the people who are looking out for every word I say, by letting them know what I really think.' There is a certain convenience in the modern and terser phrase ' off the record '.

Part of what Bismarck said was a statement of honest opinion, part pure confidence trick intended to impress Kingston with his peaceable intentions. Perhaps the most remarkable sentence in the interview was where Bismarck related the advice he had given to the Prussian generals, who he admitted were war-minded: ' You must remember, gentlemen, a war between such near neighbours and old enemies as France and Prussia, however it may turn out, is only the first of at least six.' It is a disquieting thought that, if he was right, we have only got half-way.

Whatever pleasant compliments the Iron Chancellor may have paid to Kingston's discretion when he had a story which he wanted put over, he did not like him, because his sources of information were too good and he knew too much. On one occasion only did he make an attempt to get rid of him because of his refusal to disclose certain sources of information, and when this failed owing to the intervention of the Foreign Secretary, Lord Derby, Bismarck realized that he would have to put up with this uncomfortably well-informed and independent-minded correspondent. England was still sufficiently strong to prevent the expulsion, or muzzling by threat of expulsion, of the correspondents of the country's newspapers, and dictator Press technique was far short of its later perfection. But there were no more confidential interviews.

On a later occasion Bismarck must have been considerably shaken about the serious purpose of our island race in general and of the *Daily Telegraph* Berlin correspondent in particular when in 1870 he called suddenly at the correspondents' headquarters in Versailles and found Beatty Kingston playing the piano for Sir William Howard Russell of *The Times* and Odo Russell, the Foreign Office Special Envoy, to dance the barn dance.

Kingston's position as an authority on the European scene was unchallenged until the rise to fame of Blowitz who at the time of this unfortunate discovery was acting as secretary to Laurence Oliphant, the second string of *The Times*.

However much he may have disliked him, Bismarck could not fail to recognize Kingston's pre-eminence, and found him hard to resist. Kingston had a scoop on the precise terms of the capitulation of Paris but no wire on which to send it. He asked Bismarck for the use of his official line. Bismarck told him that he must be mad to make such a request, but in the end

consented, only stipulating that the message must go un-
signed. The *Daily Telegraph* had no doubt of its origin,
attributed it, and enjoyed their ' exclusive '.

Less dynamic than Kingston but no less well suited
to his capital was Felix Whitehurst who was appointed
to Paris in 1864. He was the first regular Paris correspondent and like Kingston in Berlin he knew his capital,
its rulers, and people thoroughly well. Whitehurst
owed his success to an invincible charm both of manner
and of writing and he was particularly well suited to
describe the glitter and the colour of the Second Empire.
He was far less of a stormy petrel than Kingston and
it may be of him that the story is told of a dinner party in
London where Edward Lawson found himself next to
the wife of a British Ambassador. ' Oh, Mr. Lawson,'
she said, ' we like your correspondent so much. My
husband feels that he can always rely on him to come to
us for his information.' ' I hope I shall not have to
get rid of him ' was the quiet, deliberate, and unexpected
answer. But if it was Whitehurst the threat was not
seriously intended, for he was far too good a correspondent.

Paris was a very important news centre and Whitehurst was from time to time reinforced by men sent
temporarily from London, notably, in the early days,
James Macdonell and Hall Richardson.

Though the news editor and his function were unknown in the sixties and seventies the *Daily Telegraph*
was probably the first to guide its correspondents from
Fleet Street and indicate stories that were wanted.

Macdonell, a scholarly and sensitive Liberal, was
horrified at being charged from London to witness the
dawn execution of one of the condemned Communists.
He returned to the Paris office at ten o'clock white,
haggard, and ill.

His next task he also found distasteful, to write a review

E   55

of *La Princesse George* by Dumas Fils, which he found
' clever, witty, and corrupt, as nauseous as a bad smell '.
A more acceptable assignment was the reinterment of
Dumas Père at Villers Cotteret on which he wrote a
brilliant despatch. An interview with the Comte de
Paris on Orleanist prospects and dinner with Taine to
meet Renoir showed the variety of the work of a *Daily
Telegraph* foreign correspondent.

In the eighties, the political side of Paris appeared
to become less important and the ' Paris Day by Day '
feature made its appearance and remained one of the
attractions of the paper until the First World War. Like
most diary features, there was a good deal of scissors
and paste about it, but it was enlivened by the particular
talent and experience of the Paris correspondents.

Campbell Clarke who succeeded Whitehurst was
another of the unusual appointments. For eighteen
years he was a librarian at the British Museum. This
work, the translating of papers for the Philological
Society, and the writing of songs was a strange training
for a foreign correspondent, but he had been educated
at Bonn University, spoke several European languages
fluently, had great artistic and literary taste and knowledge, and suited well the Paris of his day. He was a
member of the jury of the two Paris Exhibitions of 1878
and 1889 and was knighted in 1897. Clarke had fortified his position at the *Daily Telegraph*, and incidentally
his bank balance, by marrying Edward Lawson's sister,
and his flat in the Place de L'Opéra became a centre of
social, literary, and artistic life. Evidence of the width
and closeness of his friendships remains in my library in
first editions of every author of his time with the warmest
personal dedications, and in some pictures from his
collection. One of these by Jean Berard, depicting Mary
Magdalene coming to Christ, with the principal politicians of the day, including Clemenceau, in frock coats

as the assembled Pharisees, was no doubt productive of
fervent discussion amongst Campbell's friends, but more
suited to the Place de L'Opéra flat of a *Daily Telegraph*
correspondent in the nineties than to an English country
house, and rather difficult to live with. At the moment,
until fashion changes, it adds a strange distinction to the
walls of my saddle-room.

Campbell Clarke served in Paris till his death in 1902
when he was succeeded after a short interval by Laurence
Jerrold, grandson of Douglas Jerrold, a man of considerable brilliance and almost equally considerable indolence,
whose scholarship and great knowledge of France well
maintained the standards of the Paris office in the easy
years between the establishment of the Entente Cordiale
and the cataclysm of 1914.

Much of what appeared in ' Paris Day by Day ', and for
that matter in the general news stories, may well have
been trivial but there is no doubt that what passed over
the Paris wire, though perhaps less vital in the scheme of
world affairs, was more readable before the main source of
information in Paris changed from the Café Napolitain to
the Quai D'Orsay.

Nor, indeed, and I can speak as a member of the Paris
staff of the time, did we miss anything of serious import.
French politics had not become a matter of particular
interest to anyone except Frenchmen, and if they were
unable to find a Government which would last more
than a few months, excessive comment then would
have been an unwarrantable intrusion into private grief.
Occasionally we were jolted, as when Madame Caillaux
shot Calmette, the Editor of *Figaro*, but that was as much
a good news story as a matter of political significance.
The politicians lived in the same calm as ourselves, and
we went on with our *faits divers*, art, music, and the
theatre, in a Europe which was still habitable by men of
simple cultured interests.

In the troubled state of foreign politics in the late sixties and for another fifteen years or so *Daily Telegraph* correspondents in many capitals may have feared every kind of invasion. That from which they were never safe was Sala. For the day-to-day coverage the *Daily Telegraph* depended on the news agencies but it was seldom that they had not a special commissioner travelling somewhere.

With the new century the foreign corps was gradually stepped up. E. W. Wilcox (afterwards in Berlin and Paris) was the first resident correspondent in St. Petersburg. Wilcox was one of the most thorough, meticulous, and conscientious of correspondents and those qualities must have made him sometimes despair of Imperial Russia though they fitted him admirably for his second assignment in Berlin.

In those days, Dillon roamed the continent on roving missions much as Sala had done before him, sometimes disturbing the peace of Europe in the Chancelleries where diplomacy was still considered a secret science, and always disturbing the peace of the resident correspondents.

Till the beginning of the First World War *Daily Telegraph* regular representation abroad was confined to the main European capitals, Paris, Berlin, and St. Petersburg, and to New York. Washington hardly attracted attention and *The Times* was the only London newspaper to have a special Washington correspondent. Percy Bullen, who for very many years represented the *Daily Telegraph* in New York and who probably knew and understood the United States better than any British newspaperman at any time, always used to say in those days that there was nothing known in Washington that was not known in New York the day before. There was more truth in this than in most exaggerations, and it was much later, and particularly with the New Deal, that Washington became a vital centre for American news.

To supplement the work of this small band of foreign correspondents men were sent specially to various countries as occasion required, supplementing the work of the agencies which formed the framework of the news.

After the 1914–18 war the resident foreign staff was again increased, but not very largely, and their work supplemented not by wandering commissioners but by the diplomatic correspondent. The first of these was Professor Gerothwohl and the circumstances of Versailles and the subsequent conferences well suited his competent and tortuous technique.

The British Foreign Office and its representatives abroad were altogether over-reticent, the missions of other European countries very expansive, and news had to be pieced together by a discounted evaluation of calculated and tendentious indiscretions. Gerothwohl's encyclopaedic knowledge of the treaties and of their makers and interpreters enabled him to keep *Daily Telegraph* readers as well and as accurately informed as possible. Now the Foreign Office and other Government departments have come to realize that if they withhold the news the Press is bound to get it elsewhere.

Modern requirements of foreign news demand a much more complete system of coverage than the old days when the jam was provided by a very small and select band of staff men and the bread and butter supplied by Reuters.

From the start, the *Daily Telegraph* attempted to make its foreign news service second to none. Le Sage may have boggled at presenting its cost to his master, but what would he think of it now? Lord Camrose put in a network of over sixty full and part-time correspondents all over the world, incurring a weekly cable bill which would have paid the whole of Le Sage's editorial salaries and left enough for Hurdell the cashier to pay the best part of the mechanical wages.

Not only in writing of the foreign correspondents but throughout this book I am concerned that I have picked out the men of old for credits, whilst the present staff, however able, are largely unmentioned.

To-day the limelight is not focused abroad on one capital more than another unless the news requires it and all the casting has to be good with consequently less opportunity for star rôles.

Small newspapers make for concentration on hard news and some of our men abroad, when they look at the files, may sigh for the greater space of the old days and the freer prospects for the brilliant pen.

Both for regular and special correspondents scoops are harder to come by and one so remarkable as Perceval Phillips's story in 1931 of the grant of oil concessions in Abyssinia is a very rare event. Then the first hint was found in London and Phillips was tipped off to get the story in Addis Ababa. The concessions do not seem to have yielded much, but the story in the troubled state of the country at the time was a good one and a real exclusive.

As with the foreign staff, so with all, the numbers are vastly greater, and the general level of excellence very much higher. There are so many of the top-class to-day that they cannot be picked out in a book of any reasonable size. Apart from that I have the haunting fear that were I to treat them as they deserve this volume might seem to be a sales promotion booklet, a fault which some similar productions have not wholly escaped.

The moderns must console themselves with the thought that if they do not stand out in the same way as did the Kingstons and the Salas amongst the lesser fry of their day it is because of the excellence of their fellows.

The qualities of enterprise and knowledge of the country of assignment remain requirements of the good foreign correspondent. What is added, or at any rate increased, is the constant vigilance which rapid communications and fierce competition make essential. Our staff abroad have the satisfaction of knowing that the reputation of the *Daily Telegraph* for foreign news which was made by occasional brilliance is maintained by thorough competence. They are writing their history to-day, and when in some years a sequel is written to this book their names may be picked out to join those few who have been mentioned in this chapter.

CHAPTER V

WAR CORRESPONDENTS

IT is a popular belief that wars are good times for newspapers. It has never been true. In war time more people buy newspapers but expenses are high and business in the advertising trades bad. All newspapers increase their circulations and the competitive position of any one is only improved so far as its service of war news is better.

Certainly in the old days wars were good times for war correspondents and the opportunities for ability and enterprise were almost unlimited.

The days of organized Press camps, conducting of correspondents' briefing conferences, and officially provided and equally shared communications were unknown. Small wars were the usual experience, and owing to the time-lag and uselessness of information to an uncivilized enemy, security was unimportant and censorship slight. Correspondents were left to their own devices and had to organize their own transport and often their own communications. The lack of system gave far greater opportunity for talent and enterprise than now when, though a good correspondent will send a better despatch than a bad one, nobody who is not idle or incompetent can fail to get a story and get it transmitted.

Frequently correspondents were better informed than the General Staff. In 1882 Godfrey Lagden was able to

give Wolseley the first information of the battle of
Kassassin. In return he asked for and got first pre-
cedence on the wires after the Government information
had been sent.

There seemed to be no settled recruiting ground for
Daily Telegraph war correspondents.

Edward Dicey is a strange candidate for inclusion in
this chapter. Dicey was a scholar and a lawyer, a Q.C.
with a great reputation as a professor of law, author of a
life of Cavour. For many years he served as a leader
writer principally writing on foreign affairs, but the
Telegraph had a habit of making unusual selections in
the hope of getting something out of the ordinary and
Dicey was sent to the Schleswig-Holstein war in 1864
and the Austro-Prussian war of 1866.

They must have seen in him more of the critic than the
news-hound for he was instructed to ' use rarely the
electric telegraph ', and indeed a survey of his messages
hardly shows that they suffered from delay.

For the Abyssinian war of 1867 the *Daily Telegraph*
made a different kind of experiment. Lord Adare,
afterwards famous as Lord Dunraven, the owner of
Valhalla, challenger for the America's Cup, was their
correspondent. Adare had no previous newspaper
experience and only such military knowledge as accrued
in a short period of service as a cornet of horse in the
Household Cavalry. Nevertheless, as a young man of
spirit and enterprise he acquitted himself well. As he
said, ' Correspondence was easy work. Mails were
infrequent and plenty of material, though not usually of a
sensational kind, was about.'

He was thoroughly well in with the staff. The
Quartermaster-General, Colonel Phayre, knew no French,
the only European language of his native interpreter, and
Adare was used as honorary interpreter and so was able
to keep close to the fountain of information.

Four hundred miles of road had to be constructed and the campaign was arduous though not unduly dangerous. The British casualties in the capture of Magdala were two killed and eighteen wounded.

Adare was well enough approved to be sent as correspondent with the Germans in the final stage of the Franco-Prussian war of 1870 but there he was only a member of a competent, professional team composed of Frank Lawley, Le Sage, and Beatty Kingston. *The Times* was also well represented by William Howard Russell and Laurence Oliphant, a most gifted man whose value as a correspondent was somewhat impaired by a conviction that he was possessed by devils.

Adare's transport was a carriage and pair which he had bought in Brussels and in which, the perfect 'milord', he drove across Europe to the scene of the conflict.

But whatever Adare may have enjoyed, Beatty Kingston urged his employer to emulate the superior magnificence of *The Times*. 'Russell has three saddle and two carriage horses, a courier, a groom in livery, an English coachman, a wagonette, splendid brougham, and a luggage waggon', he wrote to Edward Lawson, ending with the admonition 'frugality, dear old boy, on the part of newspaper proprietors so wealthy as yourselves is injudicious', and this in a letter acknowledging a draft for £200 for expenses, quite a considerable sum in those days. The efforts of specials to induce the competitive spirit in their proprietors is unchanging.

Perhaps encouraged by this favourable experience of cavalry subalterns, but more probably persuaded by Lady Randolph, Sir Edward Lawson commissioned contributions at £5 a column from Winston Churchill when he was serving in the Malakand expedition.

This sort of arrangement was common practice in smaller enterprises but major wars were reserved for the professional reporters. Bennet Burleigh would not

64

have stood for any amateurs, however gifted, encroaching on his preserves.

Like Dunraven, Bennet Burleigh in his war reporting travelled as ' milord ' with equal magnificence but less natural grace. Burleigh was the greatest of the *Daily Telegraph* war correspondents and possibly the greatest of all war correspondents. He was recruited through more normal channels. Drew Gay, who was covering the Arabi Pasha revolt in Egypt in 1882, fell foul of the military authorities and had his accreditation withdrawn. Le Sage, sent out to put the situation right, found Burleigh acting for the Central News and engaged him to replace Gay.

Burleigh was then just over forty, square built, immensely strong, tough, enterprising, aggressive and, as I remember him and others found him, rather disagreeable. A Scotsman, he had been wounded on the Confederate side in the American Civil War, taken prisoner, condemned to death and escaped. His life had been one of continual adventure. In all, he reported twenty-four wars, nearly all of them for the *Daily Telegraph*.

He saw Colonel Fred Burnaby, of ' A Ride to Khiva ', die at Abu Klea in 1885.

Half a dozen Arabs were now about him. With blood gushing in streams from his gashed throat the dauntless Guardsman leapt to his feet, sword in hand, and slashed at the ferocious group. They were the wild strokes of a proud, brave man, dying hard, and he was quickly overpowered.

Equally vivid is his description of Hector Macdonald's brigade at Omdurman :

I then saw the Dervishes for the first time in all these years of campaign turn tail, stoop and fairly run for their lives to the shelter of the hills. It was a devil-take-the-hindmost race, and the only one I ever saw them engage in through half a score of battles.

Burleigh was no stylist but his messages were incisive and vigorous. He had none of the graces of good fellowship and was never a popular man amongst his colleagues. By the war correspondents of other newspapers he was actively disliked, largely because he was fiercely, and sometimes in their view, unscrupulously competitive.

His reputation for moroseness once served the paper well. Burleigh was never known to go out of his way to express good will to anybody or to bother unduly about his family. When, therefore, on Whit-Monday 1902 Sir Edward Lawson received a message from South Africa 'Whitsuntide Greetings' and at the same time Burleigh's brother got a message 'Returning tell Lawson' it became obvious in Peterborough Court that something was up. Kitchener was then talking with the Boer leaders and there was the strictest censorship on news of the conference. The date of the cable was Whit-Sunday and the gospel of the day had 'Peace I leave with you; my peace I give unto you'. The *Daily Telegraph* next morning came out with the news that terms had been agreed. A few days later the peace was signed.

Earlier in Egypt, when Redvers Buller's column narrowly escaped annihilation in an unsuccessful attempt to relieve Gordon, Burleigh got back first to head-quarters at Korti and after filing his message to give it a good start occupied the only wire with trivia. It not only beat its competitors but also the official dispatch by twenty-four hours and the *Telegraph* came out with a special Sunday edition.

Burleigh kept himself very well informed and had a nose for trouble. After Omdurman, he travelled back with his fellow correspondents to Brindisi, accompanied them to the train, slipped away from the platform, got aboard a small Italian steamer, and returned to Cairo.

Before leaving he had heard rumours of Colonel Marchand's activities at Fashoda. There was no 'jolly old
pals' about any party of which Burleigh formed part.
He was rewarded by a scoop of Marchand's flying the
French flag at Fashoda.

In the South African War the General Staff had begun
to organize war correspondence. Burleigh was sent
there before hostilities broke out—and saw the campaign
through. He had his big Cape cart, his riding horses,
his black servants—everything in the old style—but
messages were delayed, the censorship was onerous,
and he mourned for the times that were gone. Camels
were the transport and the sands of the desert the stamp-
ing ground for the correspondent of spirit and enterprise. There was an occasional flash of the old genius.
Before actual fighting started he got into Boer country,
heard that Joubert's train was passing, and 'persuaded'
the station master to stop it. 'Evidently the sheer
impudence of the thing must have shattered him, for
he forgave me and came into the compartment, and we
chatted for hours.' He had a final triumph with his
peace scoop, but generally he was disillusioned and dis-
heartened and the fact that it was the same for all and that
no newspaper was better served was poor consolation.

Disillusionment turned to complete frustration in
the Russo-Japanese war of 1904. Burleigh was received
by the Japanese with immense politeness and consideration, so much so that he was never allowed
within earshot of a battle. This was not war-reporting
as he understood it. If his grumblings at G.H.Q. even
slightly matched his complaints to Fleet Street he
must have been an infernal nuisance. He wrote some
lively stuff from behind the lines, but it was nothing like
the old days carrying messages from square to square
at Tamai. He had seen the great days and in his view
there was no future in it.

Second in distinction of *Daily Telegraph* war correspondents was Ellis Ashmead Bartlett whose father, Sir Ellis Ashmead Bartlett, in the seventies was undercover *Telegraph* correspondent in the Russo-Turkish troubles and later caused the paper some embarrassment by chivying Dillon in the House of Commons when Dillon was in Armenia.

Ashmead Bartlett came in still another way. The others had been found in one way or another. Bartlett sold himself.

The battle of Sidney Street is remembered though its details may be forgotten. It is a story of foreign criminals and shot policemen in which a company of Guards was deployed and a Home Secretary, Mr. Winston Churchill, exposed himself to greater danger than any Home Secretary until the bombing of the Second World War.

Ashmead Bartlett had ' galloped to the sound of the guns ' and by behaviour somewhat resembling the technique of the Saint with Inspector Teal had abstracted two witnesses who were able to describe the murderers and kept them from contacts with any reporters, and incidentally with the police, until he had got his story. This he brought to the *Daily Telegraph* who gladly took it and him. What would a Press Council say to this sort of enterprise?

Bartlett covered the Balkan wars and the Italian war with Turkey and in the absence of wars travelled the world as special commissioner in the Sala manner until 1914.

Although nearly all his service was with *The Times*, the list of war correspondents would not be complete without the name of Sir William Howard Russell, Sala's thinly veiled William Bayard, ' the oldest and most famous of war correspondents and the noblest Roman of them all ' who had ' seen war in all its occasionally glorious episodes, and in all its normally hideous dirt, desolation, and despair all over the world '.

I think that Russell's single assignment for the *Daily Telegraph*, the Zulu war of 1879, came through my other grandfather, Lieut.-General Sir Frederick Marshall, who was in command of the cavalry. In this campaign Russell made criticism of the behaviour of British troops, much of which remained unanswered in Sir Garnet Wolseley's report. As in the Crimea and the Mutiny for *The Times*, here for the *Telegraph* he was always outspoken and his influence got things done. The *Daily Telegraph* possesses a peculiar by-product of Russell's service with it—a landscape of Gibraltar painted by him on his way out to Zululand.

The 1914–18 war was one of the least satisfactory for newspaper enterprise. The Service departments were groping ineffectually for a system combining military security and control with the morale-promoting benefit of keeping the nation fully informed from free and independent sources about the achievement and life of its soldiers in the field.

In the early stages, the *Daily Telegraph* made the most of its opportunities. Major Granville Fortescue, a distinguished American correspondent and author, was sent to Belgium and made the best use of such advantages as fell to a neutral. War correspondents were sent to France but none was allowed near the front. Not till August 18th were newspapers allowed to announce the landing of the British Expeditionary Force, though it was no secret here or in Germany.

Official eyewitnesses with more authority than vision were appointed, but they seemed to see very little and were fairly dumb about what little they did see.

The public were ill content and the troops in the field felt aggrieved at the scant record of their achievement, and Sir John French made representations to the War

Office. Kitchener said to Sir Reginald Brade, the permanent under-secretary, ' I do not know anything of this damned business, you look after the Press.' Brade took the view that this damned business of war reporting like most expert jobs was better done by professionals, and, in accord with this not very cordial brief, he looked after the Press to the extent of allowing them a limited number of correspondents on a pooling basis. Therefrom the *Daily Telegraph* cannot claim exclusive credit for the work of any of their war correspondents, even those who were their own staff-men such as Ashmead Bartlett in Gallipoli, G. T. Stevens in Salonica and Serbia, or W. T. Massey who was the sole correspondent in Sinai and Palestine.

Bartlett, as always, did fine work and as often got into hot water with the authorities. He sent back from Gallipoli to the Prime Minister Asquith by the hand of Keith Murdoch, then an Australian war correspondent, a private report on the situation. Someone at G.H.Q. must have heard of the letter and it was seized from Murdoch at Marseilles. So occurred the most remarkable casualty of the First World War, the loss of the letter between the War Office and Downing Street.

Sir Philip Gibbs, not a *Telegraph* man, was their chief correspondent on the Western Front and within the limits permitted to any correspondent his work was brilliant, but in the circumstances of control and organization no single paper could claim that its war reporting was outstanding.

Between the World Wars, Alan Dick, Karl Robson, and Henry Buckley did good work in the Civil War in Spain but the most distinguished war correspondent was Pembroke Stephens who was killed in action in the Sino-Japanese war.

Following 1914, much thought was given by the Service Departments, who were dissatisfied with the

First World War arrangements, to the problem of correspondence in the next war.

In the Second World War the war correspondents to some extent came back into their own. Considerations of military security, as is inevitable in large-scale conflict between civilized nations, did not permit the freedom of the small wars of the Victorian age. But within the limits of officially organized accommodation and transport and of military censorship newspapers had full accreditation for all the representatives they wanted and correspondents again became reasonably competitive. Only on certain special occasions did pooling become necessary.

Though security censorship sometimes proved irksome, the principal objection to it was rather that it did not give adequate opportunity to identify and recognize the achievements of units than that it prevented correspondents from giving the general picture of the battle. As the war progressed, commanders became more conscious of the morale value of publicity and there was considerable relaxation of restrictions, but the somewhat rigid viewpoint of the heads of military intelligence found vindication at many times and particularly at the time of the Normandy landing, when the Germans' ignorance of our battle order led them to believe that we had at least another army corps for a second landing in the Pas de Calais. It is therefore unlikely that the war correspondents in the future will enjoy much greater freedom.

In those conditions the *Daily Telegraph* employed a large number of correspondents at different times and in the various theatres of war, who did admirable work.

All might be mentioned, but I must be content with naming Christopher Buckley who was one of the two or three outstanding correspondents of British newspapers. His death by enemy action a few years later in Korea was a tragic loss.

Though there may still be the occasional opportunity for the brilliant individualist in small campaigns, as far as the major wars are concerned it would appear that the chapter of the great war correspondents is closed.

The engagement of full-time Service correspondents started with the appointment of Sir Archibald Hurd as naval correspondent at the time of the Russo-Japanese war. In recognition of his provenance, Le Sage always referred to him in the office as Togo, and persisted in so doing for many years when the Japanese admiral's name was only remembered in the reference library. Hurd served with great distinction as naval correspondent and leader-writer until in the nineteen-twenties ill-health caused his retirement. As naval correspondent he was succeeded by Hector Bywater.

The first of a line of military correspondents was Captain Battine, a cavalry officer who came to the *Telegraph* on the recommendation of Sir John French. Battine was succeeded by Colonel Repington when he left *The Times*, but the *Telegraph* only enjoyed his services when his interest had largely turned from the high strategy of war to the low diplomacy of the years that followed. He wrote at a time in international affairs when his special knowledge and talent were particularly valuable. Though his critics chose to regard him as a somewhat extinct volcano his contributions to the *Telegraph* in the comparatively short period before his death retained the distinction which characterized all that he did.

Repington's follower was that remarkable critic and publicist, Captain B. H. Liddell Hart. In Repington, the *Telegraph* were engaging a proven man, with his successor they took a chance. At the time Liddell Hart was lawn tennis correspondent and assistant military correspondent of the *Morning Post*. He was selected because of a particularly able account he had published of a rather unimportant tactical exercise.

What was the comparative extent of Liddell Hart's contribution to the success of the *Telegraph* and the *Telegraph's* contribution to the success of Liddell Hart would be a matter on which his views, as always, would be decided, if not completely uncontroversial. Given a very free hand and considerable space he soon showed the fine quality of his original mind and became a military writer of international importance.

After many years he left because, as he told me, he felt lack of scope, for Printing House Square where he did not enjoy demonstrably greater freedom and certainly had a shorter enjoyment of office. His service with the *Telegraph* was one with which the *Telegraph* was well pleased because it has always been, and always will be, their purpose to stimulate thought. Much of what Liddell Hart wrote in its columns has the same enduring value as many of his books, though it remains only for the stored files of a newspaper library.

Controversy raged then and still rages about his theories, but his great weight as a military writer can only be denied by those who only approve that with which they agree.

After Liddell Hart, the *Telegraph* made some reversion to the Repington type in that they appointed a man with a bent to political strategy.

Unlike Repington, however, General Temperley was a serving soldier who had to make the choice between Peterborough Court and command of a division. He chose Peterborough Court because he felt that his years of experience in the Disarmament Commission at Geneva particularly qualified him for the job he was asked to do at the time when he was asked to do it.

He died in harness at a time when his work was particularly important.

The Second World War saw several temporary successors until in 1943 Lieut.-General Hugh Martin was appointed.

In its shorter life, the junior Service has only had two correspondents, Major C. C. Turner who took part in the record balloon flight to Russia in 1908 and held flying certificate No. 70, and Air-Commodore Payne.

The *Daily Telegraph's* interest in Service matters began in its earliest years with the encouragement, by prizes, of rifle shooting in the Army. The plate of the Brigade of Guards and London Volunteer and Territorial Units, in particular the Honourable Artillery Company, is enriched by many Marching and Shooting Cups.

This interest has persisted throughout the paper's history and has been shown to all Services and particularly to the Territorial Army from the time of its formation. Both for Service news and military thought the *Telegraph* has always been pre-eminent.

CHAPTER VI

NIHIL HUMANUM

IT is the task of a newspaper to cover the whole field
of human endeavour, and whilst Dame Violet Mark-
ham's dictum that virtue is not news is not entirely true,
there is no doubt of the interest of newspaper readers in
the failings, misdemeanours, and crimes of their fellow
citizens. The story is surely apocryphal that the proposal of the College of Heralds for the motto of Lord
Riddell of the *News of the World* was ' nihil humanum
alienum a me puto ', though he would not be the first
or the only proprietor to realize its application in the
building of newspaper circulation.

I clearly recall the humorous incredulity of Lord
Camrose when I once told him that his paper was
founded on sensation and nearly died of respectability,
but it is not a wholly inaccurate reflection of part of
Daily Telegraph history.

The first edition of the *Daily Telegraph* records the sad
story of a widow who felt compelled to sue the Colonel
of the Grenadier Guards for the maintenance of her
illegitimate child. The case was packed with human
interest, for the unfortunate woman who was described
as ' an elegant and lady-like personage ' fainted in the
witness box, ' striking her face upon the floor with a
sickening rebound '. A year later we find the headline
' Extraordinary Discovery of a Man-Woman at Birmingham ' showing that those peculiarities of nature of

which we are occasionally reminded at our breakfast table to-day are of perennial interest to the reading public.

In typical issues of the next year we find ' Felonious Assault on a Young Female ', ' Shocking Occurrence. Five Men smothered in a Gin Vat ', ' Horrible Atrocity. A Child devoured by Pigs '; and a return to the infallible theme in ' Furious Assault on a Female '. But there was no attempt to give special typographical importance to these minor if distressing occurrences. Through the whole of this year the only headlines of any size are for the assassination of the Archbishop of Paris and for the accouchement of the Queen, and in crime stories all is straight reporting with no attempt whatever at rewriting.

Nevertheless those were the days for police court reporters. A less squeamish public had not realized the possibilities of the law of libel, judges and magistrates were less sensitive to contempts of their courts, and painters of the scene could use a broader and more faithful brush. The accused were described as ' a man of sullen aspect ' or even ' of dissolute and repulsive appearance ' or when the penman took a kindlier view ' a gentlemanly-looking man having the appearance of a foreigner '.

' What we want is a human note ' was the instruction of J. M. Levy to his young entrants. When Queen Victoria's reign became the longest of our history they recorded the quaint observation that she had outlived every member of the Jockey Club and every Master of Fox Hounds who flourished at the time of her Coronation. J. M. Levy's intention was to produce something different from other newspapers, in which politics were presumed to be almost the only interest of the reader. In pursuing this course his young men could not and did not neglect the popular interest in crime and so incurred much criticism from those who at heart were more concerned that a newspaper should gain popularity beyond the narrow circle of the hitherto well-informed than by the means by which it secured it.

One early instance of the special interest of the *Daily Telegraph* in crime was the Muller case in 1864. Muller, a young German, had murdered a man named Briggs on the North London Railway and fled to America on a sailing ship. The detectives travelled by steamer, leaving five days afterwards and arriving three weeks earlier. This excited great interest in the case and the *Daily Telegraph* sent Le Sage to Queenstown to meet the returning party. Le Sage travelled with them to Liverpool and on to London, getting a long story for which the paper published a special late edition, as the train did not get in till three in the morning. To-day, of course, there would have been a horde of reporters and cameramen at Queenstown, but then the *Telegraph* had it all to themselves.

Nobody could say that in those days the crime reporters did not see the job through. After this journey, Le Sage attended the whole of the trial and saw his man hanged outside the Old Bailey. Public executions continued until 1868.

In a somewhat similar murder in 1881 the *Daily Telegraph* again made newspaper history. Percy Lefroy or Lefroy Mapleton had murdered a wealthy man called Gold in a London to Brighton train. Because of his injuries he had been questioned by the police when he got out of the train, but his story was accepted and he disappeared. Subsequently the body of Gold was found on the line in the Balcombe tunnel but there was no Lefroy.

In the course of his inquiries for the *Telegraph* Hall Richardson was not only able to identify Lefroy with Mapleton but secured a portrait of him from his landlady. The first portrait block to appear in any newspaper in this country was the line drawing which the *Daily*

Telegraph made from this portrait. As a result of its publication Lefroy was found nine days later and arrested. Picture reproduction was not of course so perfect as to-day and no less than twenty-nine men were detained before Lefroy was finally secured.

As has been said, in all their treatment of crime, both in the early days and later, the *Daily Telegraph* confined themselves to full reporting and never made any attempt to romanticize the crime or aggrandize the criminal.

It is not the purpose of this book to examine closely the paper's treatment of crime or any other subject, but another case is deserving of special study because of the startling originality and daring of its handling by the *Telegraph*. Everything was queer about the case, even the name of the victim. In 1876 Mr. Bravo, a barrister, married to the wealthy widow of a Guards officer, collapsed with nausea after dinner at his mansion on Bedford Hill, Balham, and died in two days' time. He was seen by three doctors, including the eminent surgeon Sir William Gully. The details of the case are extremely interesting and the story is admirably told by Sir John Hall in his book of famous cases. Here we are only concerned with the case as it affects the *Daily Telegraph*.

Wife and husband were represented as a happy couple; no reason for suicide could be suggested: the Coroner did not call Mrs. Bravo and an open verdict was returned. Then Drew Gay, at the time acting chief sub-editor, got busy. He took the view that something was very fishy about the whole business, but it was dangerous stuff, and the possibilities of libel even in those less sensitive days were immense.

Gay started his inquiries and for twelve days nothing appeared, then a half-column headed ' Mystery at Balham ' disclosed that antimony in large quantity had been found at the post-mortem, that the first doctor to be called had not been subpoenaed to give evidence at the inquest, and that there was general interest locally in all these matters.

This was enough to start up a flow of information and letters to the Editor. A leading article spoke of 'the publicity we feel it our duty to give to the facts of this extraordinary affair'. Gay handled the matter with discretion but great vigour. Letters appeared from the doctors, the analyst, Bravo's father and even from the Coroner who forwarded, for the paper to publish, the depositions taken at the inquest. Public interest was red-hot and the Attorney-General adopted the extraordinary course of moving the Court of Queen's Bench to quash the inquisition, and everything was dug up, including the body of Mr. Bravo.

There was nothing hole and and corner about the second inquest. The Attorney-General, Sir John Gorst, Q.C., appeared for the Crown with Mr. Poland; George Lewis, the solicitor, for the relatives; Henry James, Q.C., afterwards Lord James of Hereford, and Mr. Biron for the widow; and two other Queen's Counsel for other persons and the Court sat for twenty-three days. And all because an interfering newspaper with an enterprising sub-editor smelt jiggery-pokery in the proceedings of a Coroner's court. The *Daily Telegraph* could not find the murderer, though Drew Gay probably had shrewd suspicions which even he dared not pursue in its columns, but they got the verdict altered to wilful murder.

Modern critics of newspaper practices might well consider this case in the question of the value of newspaper publicity to the proper administration of justice. Very curious things might occur even to-day in many kinds of courts if there were to be no publicity for their proceedings, and to be of value for this purpose there must be an adequate account of what goes on and not a formal summary of results. The fact that no murderer was brought to trial in the Bravo case does not affect the lesson. Another reflection of the student of the reports of this case might be that when we talk about the new journalism we seldom realize how little the content has changed because we are dazzled by the package. Typography and lay-out have altered the whole appearance of stories like those of the Bravo case. In the newspaper reports of to-day there would have been the occasional transatlanticisms which appear to be inseparable from any crime story, a slashing of some of the verbiage, but the essential matter would be the same. But consider how the modern sub-editor would have gloried in the opportunities for headlines and cross heads, and the general effect would be vastly more sensational. For this thrilling story the *Daily Telegraph* carried the single line heading in long primer capitals:

DEATH OF MR. BRAVO.

The interest in murder stories is and always has been almost universal. Their reading does not inspire limitation, and indeed if even more women had read the *News of the World* than do every Sunday there might have been fewer brides in Mr. Smith's baths. There is and always has been a great deal of hyprocrisy about newspaper treatment of crime. 'Disgusting the space the papers give to these cases' says the worthy citizen as he turns avidly from the *Daily X* to the *Daily Y* to see if it has a fuller story of the latest sensational murder.

At no time did the *Daily Telegraph* give space to trivial cases merely for their sordid appeal. News value was the criterion and the very considerable length of reports of criminal cases was in accord with the practice of the day, when reports of all events were of inordinate length, unless they could be dismissed in three-line snippets.

It must not be forgotten that there are unpleasant cases which any newspaper which claims to be complete cannot avoid reporting. I have heard it said by an old friend with long memory that the circulation of the *Daily Telegraph*, which in its old age claims to be a ' quality ' newspaper, even in its middle age was largely built on specially full reports of these cases, and he instanced the Oscar Wilde trial. He would be surprised if he looked at the files. That space should be given to this case was inevitable. The literary and social eminence of Wilde made any sort of playing down impossible and the formidable array of counsel and Wilde's brilliant and self-destroying evidence made inescapable copy. The record shows that in three days of the Queensberry libel action the *Telegraph* had ten columns, in the first criminal trial seven and a quarter columns in five days, and in the second trial two and a quarter columns in six days whilst that supposed pillar of respectability, *The Times*, had six and a half, four and a quarter, and three columns for the three actions. The duty of every newspaper is to report the news of the day and nothing is reprehensible except undue selectivity.

Reviewing the files, the honest biographer cannot dispute that the *Daily Telegraph* thrived on crime. So did, does, and will every newspaper, but the reformers must realize that when crime is not reported in a way that will attract the reader it will not be reported at all. Then, with the millennial control of the Press by the faddists, will come the opportunity for the weak-minded to indulge their petty vices and for more serious criminals to operate without fear of public knowledge of themselves and their methods.

That being said in defence of the full reporting of crime, the honest biographer must also admit that in its early days the *Daily Telegraph* sometimes overdid it.

The Rugely poisoning case in 1856 had five leaders and on one day the report filled a quarter of the paper, but there was continuing purpose in full coverage and comment as after the verdict the *Daily Telegraph* maintained that the verdict was improper and that the jury was biased against Palmer. In 1864, the hanging of Catherine Wilson, the first woman to be executed for ten years, got three columns of detailed description.

Jack the Ripper in 1888 brought copious reports, of course, but no fuller than they would be to-day in every paper in the land, and the *Daily Telegraph* went deeper than reporting a series of sordid murders. It examined the lives of the wretched women who were the victims and put the landlord in the dock of public opinion.

' The owners of property are too strong for you! Property! Property gets money from lodging houses which spread nameless vice, nameless crime, nameless disease; property lets men and women live worse than troglodytes '—good strong stuff for a conservative paper appealing to comfortable people.

That the *Daily Telegraph* was conscious of a certain over-concentration on the unpleasant is shown by a persistent sensitivity: ' We are to a certain extent the guardians of public morality, and the censor of the impudent vice which occasionally insists upon thrusting itself in the light of day '; ' All we could do was to suppress as much of the grosser indecency of the evidence as lay in our power '; ' We are thoroughly convinced that, on the whole, public morality gains by the notoriety given to crime through the medium of full and fair reports of all legal proceedings.' There was honest conviction as well as self-comfort in this last reflection. In the papers of the day there was plenty of suppression, sometimes from good motives but not always, and the upstart felt a plain duty to publish all the news pleasant and unpleasant, and particularly to resist all pressure to omit what was unpalatable to persons of wealth and influence.

Samuel Butler, as a writer of fiction, should not perhaps be put in the witness box, but novels reflect the life of their day and readers of the *Way of all Flesh* will remember that when Towneley asked the reporters to keep Ernest's case out of the newspapers ' he was successful as regards all the higher class papers. There was only one journal, and that of the lowest class, that was incorruptible'. Of course any paper not amenable to the requests of persons of position must be ' of the lowest class ', but the adjective is ' incorruptible '.

If the *Telegraph* was somewhat on the defensive about its attitude to lesser matters in the courts, on major crime it was frankly and resolutely unrepentant: ' He is a shallow critic who wonders at the public interest in great crime, and finds fault with it. There is something far deeper than the vulgar love of startling incidents in this universal emotion.'

The *Daily Telegraph* treatment of divorce was easy to understand. It must be remembered that divorce in the law courts only became possible two years after the foundation of the paper. Previously a marriage could only be broken by special Act of Parliament, machinery available to few but the rich and privileged. As the *Telegraph* sententiously observed, ' the new divorce court is a cosmoramic exhibition of all that is miserable in parlours and drawing-rooms '. But, miserable or not, it was new and it was news.

The misery of parlours had only a passing news interest, the misery of drawing-rooms had a longer life as a reader attraction, and in the middle years the amount of space given to divorce cases was judged far more by the social prominence of the parties than by any particular ' spiciness ' of the evidence. That evidence was frequently frank and revealing, but a plain statement by a domestic or hotel servant that two persons, one at least married to someone else, slept in the same bed, though distressing to the moralist, can hardly be called salacious or, to use the popular modern term, pornographic.

The legislation which now governs the reporting of divorce cases may well have had most excellent results, but it was bred by Puritanism out of Muddled Thinking.

The most unpleasant court cases involving sex are not divorce cases at all, and their reporting is subject to no restriction.

And there is another side to it. The confining of reports to the barest detail has resulted in the almost complete disappearance of reports at all except of persons of special prominence and has removed a considerable deterrent to recourse to the divorce courts. Few people to-day can want to keep together the hopelessly unsuitable, but many marriages could be happily saved by a little more effort by the parties to make a success of them, and especially where there are children this is not without value.

Certainly the publicity given to divorce by the *Daily Telegraph* and other papers in the last twenty years of last century and the first ten of this was much more calculated to inspire dislike of the divorce court than to attract readers to adultery. Without any special pleading for the old system of divorce court reporting, the newspaperman reviewing old practice and modern behaviour may be excused a reflection that publicity was not entirely reprehensible.

But the purpose of this volume is historical and not to air the peculiar opinions of the author, and so on with factual review.

The first really sensational divorce to be reported at great length was the Mordaunt case in 1870, and that this should have been reported not only in the *Daily Telegraph* but in every paper was unavoidable.

The unfortunate Lady Mordaunt had made wild confessions of infidelity with a number of men including a peer, a baronet and Member of Parliament, and the heir to the Throne. The Prince of Wales was able to go into the witness box and deny the accusation on oath and the court found that the lady was insane.

The hearing was in Westminster Hall and at one stage in the trial the gallery had to be surveyed to discover whether it could bear the weight of onlookers. It was very much a case where it was desirable that there should be full publicity. The judge, Lord Penzance, in his summing-up observed ' Many-tongued rumour gave its account of those who were implicated in it, and while reports are spread around floating about in all classes of society, is it altogether an evil that we should come into the open day, and investigate the matter, and to remedy a part of the wrong that has been done ? '

With all the legal restrictions on divorce court reporting, the case to-day would have been infinitely more sensationalized than in the straight reporting with a simple small headline and no cross heads of the papers of 1870. And what would ' many-tongued rumour ' say to-day of what transpired in court and could not be made public?

The next big case which brought particular criticism of *Daily Telegraph* reporting length was the Colin Campbell case in 1886. This was the first time that legal restriction of divorce court reporting was strongly suggested. Mr. Justice Butt at the commencement of his summing-up deplored the reports of the cases and in another place Sir Creswell Creswell, the president of the divorce court, advocated that cases should be heard in camera.

The *Daily Telegraph* had in all sixty-two columns on a

trial that lasted seventeen days, but every daily paper in the country was almost equally full. It was the prominence of the parties, not the unsavoury nature of some of the evidence, which made this inevitable at the time; the son of a duke was one of the principals; the other four co-respondents were a second duke, the head of the London Fire Service, a general who was the husband of a famous artist, and a leading London physician. The Attorney-General and the Solicitor-General represented two of them and Queen's Counsel of equal eminence appeared for others concerned on both sides.

Some of the unpleasant evidence is reported with such reticence as to be almost incomprehensible to the reader to-day. The *Daily Telegraph* expressed its cordial agreement with a letter signed by a number of eminent men urging the limitation of divorce reports.

But no action was taken and the *Telegraph* with other papers continued to do ' its public duty to give a fair account of such painful proceedings as these ' and their ' equal duty to render such reports as little offensive as circumstances permit '.

The two Hartopp cases in the new century have been adduced by *Daily Telegraph* critics as evidence that the paper's excessive interest in divorce persisted into the twentieth century. In fact, *Telegraph* reporting was no fuller than that of other papers and the social prominence of those concerned caused great interest in the cases in which there were no more sordid and unpleasant details than in any story of marital misbehaviour.

Having in the course of my researches over a considerable period read a great deal of *Telegraph* divorce court reporting with at least as low a mind and as pure a heart as the average reader, I fail to find anything lewd or provocative.

To-day, were all restrictions on report removed I

The *Daily Telegraph* machine-room in 1865

Part of the machine-room in 1945. The reel on the right is being lowered to the basement for the magazine-feeding of the machines

George Augustus Sala
From *Vanity Fair*, September 25th, 1875

would use the blue pencil with devastating ferocity, but more with the thought that it is all so very unimportant and that newsprint is £50 a ton than that its publication would cause any deterioration in public or private morals. I fail to find that this pitiless and overfull recital can have produced any incentive to disregard the marriage bond but, on the contrary, by the perhaps undesirable means of exposure it may have been a deterrent.

If the purpose of any newspaper were to select what is unpleasant in sex to gratify the supposed tastes of readers, they had then and have now ample opportunity without touching divorce. If restriction is based on the argument that the incompatibilities and the warm-hearted sins of individuals should have the protection of a certain privacy then it has at least partly accomplished its purpose, but if it is to guard the eyes of the innocent from what they are better not reading it has only changed the subject from one form of unpleasantness to another.

In surveying this part of the field a descendant of the founders must freely admit that in some respects they were not very idealistic but eminently practical. Never in their plans at any time was their high purpose in doubt. They were very clear-minded about their intention for their content, a wider field of home news with a human touch, a literary quality generally inconspicuous in the Press of their day, provision for the cultural interests of the newly educated public, and an extensive and efficient foreign service through their own correspondents. This comes out again and again, not in pronouncements for public consumption but in internal letters and memoranda.

The circulation to pay for these ambitious and praiseworthy aims had to be achieved somehow, and if ' human interest ' had to be hotted up a bit to finance the long-term programme of perfection they were not going to be foolishly narrow-minded about it. They were practical men but there was no doubt about their high aim and sound intention. The end may or may not have justified the means, which anyway were not very improper. Family pride, however, does not justify humbug.

And it must not be forgotten that often when in pursuit of human interest the *Daily Telegraph* incurred the horrified censure of the old-fashioned it was for stories that to-day would hardly raise an eyebrow in the reading-room of the Athenaeum. Fashions and readers' judgments change with the years and the quality of horror is not unvarying. The *Daily Telegraph* of 1861 comments on the practice of Miss Rachel Nevison, a cosmetician, 'What a horrifying discovery it would be to find that one's wife was enamelled.' To some to-day it would be at least a revealing experience to see her when she was not. And I will end this chapter on a still lighter note.

Many and varied were the special features of the *Daily Telegraph*. The sponsoring of enterprises of discovery and adventure are elsewhere recorded in this book, as are the development of special and worthwhile silly-season correspondence. These were sound and interesting, but *Telegraph* readers should know that it was not immune from less creditable promotions of the trivial, and as evidence that their old and trusted newspaper in its youth was, like Habbakuk, '*capable de tout*', I produce without evasion, equivocation, or reservation of any kind the story of Jumbo.

Those who consider that the *Daily Mail* and Lord Northcliffe were the originators of newspaper stunts should have a look at the *Daily Telegraph* of 1882. Sweet peas and funny hats have nothing on Jumbo.

Jumbo was the favourite elephant at the Zoo on

which thousands of children had ridden. He became
a trifle bad-tempered and the Fellows sold him to
Barnum for £2,000.

Godfrey Turner, one of the most attractive of writers
and enterprising of men, was put on to the story. Letters
from grown-ups and children flowed in by every post,
parcels and gifts of buns and cakes poured into the
gardens. The principal actor played his part nobly by
refusing to enter the travelling cage to take him to the
docks.

Sex raised its fragrant head, for Turner discovered
that there was a female elephant called Alice whom
Jumbo refused to leave.

The Zoo was crowded out and Scott, the keeper,
became a national figure. A song beginning ' Jumbo
said to Alice, I love you ', swept the halls, the sweet
manufacturers sold vast quantities of Jumbo Rock and
of a horrible liquorice confection called Jumbo's Chains,
and financed by public subscription (not organized by
the *Daily Telegraph*) an injunction was sought in the law
courts to prohibit the sale.

Mr. Justice Chitty, with traditional judicial disregard
of popular clamour, laid down wisely and simply that
if the Royal Zoological Society could buy an elephant
they could also sell one, and so Jumbo crossed the
ocean to meet his death by getting in the way of an
express train.

CHAPTER VII

FIRST AUTUMN

FROM 1880 to the end of the century was the autumn of the first generation of proprietors and as is usual with autumns it was a season of mellow fruitfulness. Opinion had appreciably mellowed and publisher and advertisement manager were bringing in the golden harvest.

In 1870 a six months daily average circulation was 196,855, in 1877 it had risen to 242,215 and shortly afterwards it was announced that:

> The proprietors have erected entirely new buildings with vastly improved machinery capable of printing 168,000 copies per hour, every copy being Bound, Cut, and Folded, so that henceforth there will appear advertisements and News Always Together . . . appearing as a rule in Ten Page and every Saturday Morning a Twelve Page Paper.

The larger paper on Saturday, contrary to modern practice, was due to the introduction of what we should now call magazine features for week-end reading which distinguished the *Daily Telegraph* from its competitors. In 1875, Sir Edwin Arnold calculated that a year's issues of the *Daily Telegraph* placed end to end would reach the moon.

In June, 1875, appears a whole-page advertisement, though still in columns, of Clarke's World-Famous Blood Mixture. Next month there is an 'Inventor's

Column' at seven shillings for three lines and two shillings for every additional line. Inventions include 'a new watchman's detector clock', 'a patent central fire walking stick', and 'Armstrong's portable chair lounge—folds up into a book'. In 1896 a rate of ten shillings and sixpence a line is announced for Society and Fashionable paragraphs.

In the eighties there were a number of full-page advertisements still arranged in columns. The first real display advertisement is in 1887 for the new Lancashire, Derbyshire, and East Coast Railway headed by a large map of the area covered by the service. The displayed announcements of Harrods and Vinolia soap appear about this time. Harrods had the first double-page spread for the opening of their new buildings in 1896, the year in which the first sixteen-page paper appeared.

The paper is packed with advertising and though there is no indication of rates, as far as can be ascertained they were about two shillings a line.

The news service has been thoroughly organized and developed so that we have, as Sala describes, the daily intake of the Morning Mammoth:

> Wars and rumours of wars, the price of gold at San Francisco, the depreciation of the rupee at Calcutta, corners in pork and grain at Chicago and in Erie railroad shares in New York, coal miners and trainworkers strikes, a famine in Russia, a beer riot at Munich, a balloon accident at Rangoon, a kidnapping by brigands in Sicily, an anti-clerical demonstration in Rome, an attack on missionaries at Shanghai, a diplomatic ball at Pekin with a full explanation of the political motives which prompted the Russian Minister to have an attack of measles on the very evening previous to the British plenipotentiary's dance.

Not only the foreign news but home news previously received by mail is telegraphed.

Hard news is supplemented by background material and descriptive writing by travelling special commissioners, Sala and others, and by feature articles ranging from sporting reminiscences by the Hon. Francis Lawley to 'Men, Cities and Events' by Beatty Kingston. Both of these were staff men, as were the authors of the greater part of this kind of material. Articles from contributors are rare.

Special features are frequent. In 1872 the *Daily Telegraph* by many years anticipated the B.B.C. with a special programme called ' Christmas Round the World ', a series of telegraphic greetings from English residents from Christiana to Japan enabling, as the *Telegraph* proudly announces, ' the entire British community to shake hands on Christmas morning '.

In great happenings its news service was outstanding. In 1873 it had the news of the fall of Khiva long before any other paper. Nor did it neglect the lighter side and in the same year it first discovered the Loch Ness Monster. Altogether it was a paper better informed and lighter than anything else available to the Victorian reader and, as the circulation figures showed, demonstrably preferable.

Opinion both on political and general topics had mellowed. On the political side this was due to the fact that Edward Lawson was actuated at this time by what could fairly be called both independence of mind and confusion of thought.

The *Telegraph* was traditionally Liberal and even when it changed to support of the Conservatives it was still, as it always has remained, a paper of liberal views. It was depressed by the disorganization and lack of efficiency of the Liberal Party and as early as 1868 it said sharply, ' What the Liberals eminently need is a good drill sergeant.' It is remarkable how unchanging are politics.

The first notification of possible secession was on a trivial issue of a proposal in 1872 by Jacob Bright to reduce defence expenditure.

' All we can say is that if the Liberal Party shares the opinions of Mr. Jacob Bright, the sooner we have a Tory majority and a Tory Government the better for this ancient and high-spirited people.'

More serious matters widened the rift, Gladstone's treatment of the Alabama claim, the Church Regulation Bill, and finally the two great issues of Irish and Eastern policy. Gladstone ' has aided more powerfully than any other man save the Czar in plunging South East Europe and a large part of Asia into an ocean of un-imaginable suffering '. He would ' fling half our Empire overboard and jettison India herself in order to teach Britain modesty '. Well might Gladstone, when he visited Lawson and Le Sage, have thought that they were of set purpose.

Still, except when Arnold's orientalism ran away with his pen, their attitude to Gladstone was neither un-varyingly nor immoderately hostile.

Outside politics, the Pre-Raphaelites had become almost respectable. The *Daily Telegraph* can write of ' mature and sensible Pre-Raphaelitism—Pre-Raphaelit-ism in fact with its hair cut and its face washed'. Whistler has receded in *Telegraph* esteem since the ' Symphony in White ' was allowed ' to gleam on the wall like an opal '.

In matters of painting it would not be unfair to say that the *Telegraph* judgments more reflected the opinion of the time than cast light on the past or on the future of art.

A Turner fetched under £2,000 at the same sale at which Edwin Long's ' Babylonian Marriage Market ' was sold for 6,300 guineas. ' Despite the heathenish custom which it depicts it bears the stamp of quiet

British propriety.' It must be a quaint picture and I wonder where it is.

In drama there was little change at the *Telegraph* though much new in the theatre. The *Telegraph's* view of Wilde may have been cradled in prejudice but possibly was not unsound. Of *Lady Windermere's Fan:* ' The play is a bad one but it will succeed. No faults of construction, no failure of interest, no feeble-ness of character drawing, no staleness in motive will weigh in the scales against the insolence of its caricature.'

By the young Shaw, the *Telegraph* seems to be too puzzled to pass judgment. Ibsen is exposed to the full blast of Scott's intolerance. Clement does not like ' men and women without a spark of nobility in their nature, men without conscience and women without affection, an unlovable, unlovely and detestable crew ', and that is that.

Wagner is the chief musical headache which is finally alleviated by the aspirin of thought that ' a Wagner, like a Napoleon, comes far less often than the aloe blossoms, and when he goes the things that he has turned topsy-turvy right themselves with marvellous facility ', and when they did the *Telegraph* could get down to the job of noticing less provocative music for an increasing musical public. By the end of the century it had four full-time staff critics.

Architecture too seldom attracts the attention of the critics to enable one to form much view of *Telegraph* taste. The Albert Hall ' has the general appearance of a Stilton cheese, crowned by a dish cover, of a stable for locomotives or a piano manufactory at Camden ' but rather surprisingly in view of this the Albert Memorial is ' a noble and all but perfect piece of commemorative building. . . . From the still and stately company of white figures at the spreading base, to the mounting pinnacles and the angels and the Holy Cross, the work is beautiful '.

In literature, it could not take the Yellow Book and Aubrey Beardsley, but it welcomed Hardy and Kipling. The story that it blindly failed to recognize the new genius of Kipling is entirely based on Edward Lawson's refusal to publish ' Barrack Room Ballads ' in the paper. Is it not possible that he was right in finding them unsuitable for serial publication in a daily paper?

On other issues of the day the *Daily Telegraph* was sometimes reactionary but often far in advance of contemporary opinion.

It opposed the Channel tunnel on the limited strategic concept that ' we should have enough to do, without being obliged to watch over the English end of a submarine tunnel like a terrier over a rat hole '.

But it also opposed the M'Naghten rules on grounds that read strangely in a world which knew not the psychiatrist; and its views on the effect of bad housing on crime were curiously modern in days when papers largely wrote for the propertied classes.

It advocated the metric system and open-air parks in London. Its views on the ' Abominable Saturnalia of Guy Fawke's day ' can frequently be read in Novembers of to-day.

And all the time the news collecting system which had been fully established in the first period was progressively strengthened and extended. News from all quarters at home and abroad was supplemented by feature articles, not only on Saturday, the big ' magazine ' day, but on every day of the week.

James Greenwood—'One of the Crowd '—with stories of the London underworld; Clark Russell—' Seafarer '—with the yarns told him by sailors; Phil Robinson with sketches of the Zoo; Arnold when on his travels;

Beatty Kingston from all over Europe; and from everywhere and on everything, Sala.

Book reviews became more and more systemized, generally six on the special day with at least two novels.

The columns looked fairly solid, but compared with those of competitors they were lightened by maps in war reports and foreign and other special articles, illustrating everything from boundary disputes to the Boat Race. Illustrations began in December, 1879, with a sketch of the Tay Bridge as it was before the disaster, and in 1884 the first war pictures in any daily paper, a sketch by Melton Prior of the battle of El Teb.

Any good portrait has an element of caricature because it is the peculiarities of the subject which stamp the likeness. I have the thought that in the portraiture of this book, and particularly in some of the quotations, I have overdone the idiosyncrasies and failed to make plain not only what a readable but what a good newspaper the *Daily Telegraph* was.

It wants a lot of knowledge or a lot of imagination, or both, to understand how a newspaper starting from nothing in a very few years can have achieved a position which has never been enjoyed by a single newspaper before or since.

And to understand this, one must think about the times in which it happened. The Crimean War and the Mutiny had passed but the next forty years were packed with wars and rumours of war; the American Civil War, the Austro-Prussian war, the Liberation of Italy war of 1870, the Russo-Turkish war, Egypt and the death of Gordon and the revenge of Omdurman, the Matabele and Zulu wars, and countless frontier wars in India— as far as England was concerned all small wars, but small wars are the only wars that ordinary men can follow and understand. And all, both great and small, were covered by the *Daily Telegraph* with brilliant correspondents and an expenditure on organization and cabling on a scale unprecedented for any paper in the country.

Africa was a largely undiscovered and vastly exciting continent and the *Daily Telegraph* took a lead in its exploration.

Science was progressing swiftly and surprisingly. The effective growth of the railways was in this period, which also saw the electric telegraph, the telephone, and at the end in a still small way the internal combustion engine.

Science may be progressing even more swiftly and surprisingly to-day, and flight and television may be more remarkable developments than anything our grandfathers knew. But our grandfathers were more susceptible to surprise and did not greet inventions with the blasé indifference which considers just a new gadget anything less than the hydrogen bomb. The *Telegraph* never forgot Thornton Hunt's early directive about the reader interest of science.

And those were the days when politics were politics with big issues dividing the parties, the reform bills, the Irish question, no common platform on foreign affairs, all in a House where there was real debating and not the delivery of set and prepared addresses.

They are thrilling times to read about; how much more thrilling they must have been to live in. And they were times when the public first felt a thirst for news, not only from their own country but from the whole world, which the *Daily Telegraph* gave them in fuller measure than any paper except *The Times* whose circulation did not extend widely below Olympus. This thirst was accompanied by hunger for information of all that was new in science, literature, art, and the theatre, and for that matter much that was old but which they did not know because they were newly educated and books were out of their reach.

All this accounts for the success of the *Telegraph*. What is more difficult to understand is its popularity measured by other standards than circulation. There are papers with larger circulations, and there are papers with greater revenues. These are facts. There may be papers that are wiser and better informed and with greater influence. These are opinions which I do not happen to share, but of one thing I am certain—that there is no paper in this country for which its readers had and have a deeper affection. I do not ask anyone to take this from me but only to inquire of newsagents. Readers of other papers may like them or admire them, but they have not for them the feeling which makes them speak of the *Telegraph* as ' the good old *D.T.*' This is an attitude which may bring and at times has brought a danger of complacency, but one which it is very pleasant to experience. And it is an attitude which began very early. The *Telegraph* gratified this hunger and thirst for news and information and it very soon recovered from its early extravagances and became what Lord Camrose later advertised, ' The paper you can trust.' And it told all this in a way which the people could understand. The turgid and portentous ' Telegraphese ' which excited the scorn of Matthew Arnold was the language of the stars, news was reported in reasonably plain and straightforward style, and the stars were the stars and had to be allowed to sparkle even if rather artificially.

Its leaders expressed the thought of most of its readers better than they could express it themselves, and sometimes inspired them to higher thought and greater endeavour which, as good citizens, they welcomed. It was seldom anything but constructive and did not overdo the preaching.

But above all, the *Daily Telegraph* recognized that they were interested in new things and told them about new

things in a new way, and by 1880 some quarter of a
million of them bought it. And more and more they
bought it until someone began to tell them about new
things in a newer way and for less money.

On May 4th, 1896, Alfred Harmsworth brought out
the *Daily Mail* at a halfpenny a copy.

CHAPTER VIII

STARS OF THE EVENING

BRIDGING the gap between the Victorians and the Georgians comes W. L. Courtney. It is remarkable how often the *Daily Telegraph* went to the Universities, not for ordinary graduates but for scholars of distinction.

Most of them shed their academical cloak when they entered its doors but Courtney always retained a somewhat donnish approach to the most mundane problems.

After the ebullient and sometimes shallow omniscience of Sala and the rampageous enthusiasms and prejudices of Scott, Peterborough Court must have found him a strange, gentle, learned creature, and felt blowing through its passages a gentle zephyr after the raging East and North winds. Courtney had greater depths and clearer judgments but he was not as good a journalist as either of the men whose place he largely took.

The paper which he served had become in some ways more distinguished but in many less forceful and vigorous.

Courtney was forty years old before he left New College for Peterborough Court in 1890 and he continued in the service of the *Telegraph* until he died six years after the First World War. Co-founder with Arthur Bourchier of the Oxford University Dramatic Society he was also Editor of the *Fortnightly Review*, a more cultured apprenticeship than the *Household Words* of Sala. He succeeded Clement Scott for a time as dramatic critic but his principal work for the *Telegraph* was as leader writer and literary editor. He was a man of profound reading and a philosopher but well capable *in loco* of providing for the lighter interests of *Telegraph* readers with a somewhat ponderous grace. To the student of the files those of his contributions which are signed or identifiable read well and interestingly even to the changed judgments and tastes of to-day, but much of his value to the paper was not in what he wrote.

The departure of Arnold at the end of the century left a real gap. Le Sage was no whale for culture and in the editorial counsels the scholarly, artistic, but not un-wordly wisdom of Courtney provided something for the daily plan which was sadly wanting, particularly as at this time Lord Burnham was spending more time at Hall Barn and Harry Lawson was busy in the House of Commons.

Early in his *Telegraph* career Courtney brought back something of the invigoration of the North wind by importing J. L. Garvin from the *Newcastle Chronicle*. Garvin was something new for the *Telegraph*. Most of the stars of the past had been romantics and several of them had been poets, not great ones but no worse than at least one Laureate of the day. Garvin's descrip-tive prose was florid and rhetorical but he was no romantic. His articles of opinion had a sustained and practical ferocity, more convincing than the rodomon-tades of the eighties. His first important assignment was the funeral of Queen Victoria. Probably his best descriptive work was the Coronation of Edward VII and his despatches from India during the visit as Prince of Wales of George V.

Garvin only served a few years before he left to edit the *Outlook* but in that time, both as descriptive writer and leader writer, he was a sensible force.

The young lions who survived were getting long in the tooth and Garvin's work did much to bring back the old vitality. He was master of the long article, though when there was beginning to be less place in the daily paper for the long article. Far the greatest of the second generation of lions, his ambition was to be a lion-tamer with freedom to roar himself, and editorship of the *Outlook* was only a step to the greater opportunities of the *Observer*. Garvin's fault as a daily newspaper writer was his prolonged questing for the right word and his reluctance to accept the second best. He was therefore a slow writer and he revelled in space.

Frivolity is excusable about the truly great. S. J. Glanville, later assistant editor, asked suddenly for his most vivid recollection as a sub-editor of Garvin said, ' A make-up comp searching the room for a lost galley and crying, " Where's number five of bloody everlasting ? " '

None of the brilliant men who served the *Telegraph* in its long history wrote with greater distinction. The Garvin story had a particularly pleasing ending. When differences with the proprietor caused Garvin's retirement from the editorship of the *Observer* he was engaged to write regular leader page articles for the *Daily Telegraph*. This engagement gratified Lord Camrose's strong sense of *Telegraph* tradition, his admiration of a great writer bereft of a public, and his personal regard for the man. To Garvin it gave immense pleasure to end where he had begun in London journalism, an arrangement reflecting credit on all concerned and of marked advantage to *Daily Telegraph* readers.

Perceval Landon came from *The Times* to the *Telegraph* and served it for twenty-five years until his death in 1927. Landon was one of the roving correspondents of high distinction whose work, in accord with *Telegraph* practice of the time, filled in the framework of the news.

Sir Edward Lawson in the editorial chair

The opening of the new offices, June, 1882

The Prince of Wales is seated at the table with the Duke of Albany on the right; facing him stand Mr. and Mrs. Edward Lawson

In 1905 he covered the Prince of Wales's journey to India and for the next six years journeyed through Persia, Nepal, Russia, Turkestan, Egypt, and the Sudan. In 1911 he was the *Telegraph* correspondent at the Delhi Durbar and after the war accompanied another Prince of Wales on a tour of India.

In the West, he had a brief experience as a war correspondent at St. Omer and was the leader of the *Daily Telegraph* team at the Versailles Conference.

The East was his province and he wrote of it with rare knowledge and understanding. Reading Landon in these days, it is perhaps surprising to find that a travelling correspondent of an ordinary daily newspaper should have attempted a description of the Taj Mahal in its columns. I give an extract as a sample of Landon's style and as an example of the occasional gems that in the nineteen-hundreds could be found in the setting of a prosaic journal.

Other buildings in the world have their own personal identity, their own attitude towards the ways and loves of men. St. Mark's challenges the inner lives of men, St. Peter's the crooking of their knees, the Pyramids confront the rising and the setting sun, the pole star and all the celestial company, Salisbury gazes coldly and very certainly upwards into heaven. The Taj Mahal alone crouches together, still huddled in loveliness and utter misery, crying only to be left alone with her dead. There is no front to the Taj; go where you will, she turns away, and will have none of the world's consolation, its sympathy, or, worst of all, its admiration. Blind with her own tears, she dwells apart, the spirit of love incarnate, realizing to the bitter dregs the uselessness of raising jewelled homes of marble for the unresponsive dead. Arjumand is dead, is dead, and not all the wealth of him who never had an earthly rival in splendour can buy back one fleeting hour. It is misery made manifest.

That was Landon.

E. C. Bentley wrote such admirable leaders for the *Telegraph* in the first quarter of the twentieth century that it seems hardly right that he should be remembered to-day more as the composer of Clerihews and the author of the best detective novel in the English language. It shows how short is the memory for good newspaper work.

H. C. Bailey (*D.T.* 1902–46) also had the misfortune of having created a novel character on whom his literary reputation rests. His work as a writer of the parliamentary sketch and of the last light leaders was anonymous and therefore unknown.

J. B. Firth (*D.T.* 1897–1943) more often wrote under signature in the paper. Firth went straight from Oxford into the editorial chair of the *Lancashire Evening Post* and soon came to London. Le Sage, always profoundly suspicious of intellectuals, thought that a good breaking-in for a first in Greats would be the editing of the Woman's Page and, as an alternative, writing the news summary. But Le Sage could not keep a good man down, nor did he want to once he had got a proper sense of proportion into a classical scholar and ex-editor coming into Fleet Street.

Firth's interest was politics and particularly home politics. He had the understanding of a close student, the knowledge of a historian, and a great gift of style and lucid expression. Firth's leaders, which carried well into Lord Camrose's time, were *Daily Telegraph* opinion at its soundest and best.

His best piece of descriptive writing was of the funeral of King Edward VII in St. George's Chapel. I give a quotation as a contrast to an earlier purple passage of Dillon's.

> Who can resist the sight of those avenues of gorgeously-painted banners, hanging stiff and square above the slender, lace-like canopies of the fifteenth-century stalls, banners

never stirred by a breath of wind, though the devices they bear suggest battle and the shock of knightly war? Looking down from these, from the crowns, the coronets, the gilded helmets and the swords, drawn just sufficiently from the golden scabbards to show the duller glint of steel, the eye was lost amid the traceries of the canopies, on which the dust lay thickly, and imparted a curious pearly sheen till it fell on the brass plates of the knights attached to the backs of their stalls, richly engraved and enamelled, and lighting up the dark of the ancient oak. . . .

The guns boomed out their dull reverberations, the hateful bell tolled on. The King, the dead King was coming ever nearer. Open they fling the big door of the nave, looking down upon the flight of steps, and the glory of the strong sunshine which made even the lucent nave less bright. What a picture! Framed in the doorway was the verdant grass of the Horse Shoe Cloisters, and we could see the stalwart figures of the Scots Guards, with the officers restlessly walking to and fro—waiting, even as we were waiting, for the coming of the King. Birds flew by the open door in the warm air; butterflies played in the light.

T. P. O'Connor gets his place in this chapter because though he was one of the early staff his chief work for the *Telegraph* was done in the later years. He was one of the greatest journalists of all time but his reputation was formed elsewhere.

His share in the few years for which he served after joining the staff in 1876 was slight and no record remains of it but the story of J. M. Levy looking at his expense sheet with its ' Cab 5/- ', ' Cab 5/- ', ' Cab 10/- ' and observing, ' This can't be right, why doesn't this young man sometimes pay 4/6 and 7/6 ', a thought which has sometimes occurred to J.M.L's great-grandson when scrutinizing the claims of some of T.P.'s successors.

In his old age T.P. came back to the *Telegraph* as a contributor particularly in the somewhat specialized field of anticipating the news requirement of the last enemy. Frequently having failed with the Editor, he would come and see me about the urgency of certain work. Much snuff was consumed and much agreeable conversation enjoyed, but I was generally left with the impression that the urgency was more concerned with the state of T.P.'s finance than the health of his subjects. The arrangement was always for payment at space rates on receipt of the copy.

Consequently, some twenty-seven years ago Lord Camrose became the possessor of copious files of lengthy tributes to a number of eminent men and women who enjoyed many years of fruitful life and some of whom are I trust, despite advanced age, reading this book with pleasure and in the enjoyment of good health. I can only assure their relatives that when their great kinsfolk in God's good time receive a shorter tribute from another pen it will be due to T.P.'s death and the newsprint shortage and to no altered assessment of their merit.

Much of his work at this time, particularly when he wrote of men he knew well, was brilliant and T.P. obituaries were a great attraction of the *Daily Telegraph*.

This chapter purports to tell of some of the stars of the later period of the first régime. There are names not included in it which are elsewhere mentioned. There are many others who might well merit inclusion but a selection has to be made and I have no particularly guilty conscience about notable omissions. That may come when others read the work, and accuse me of carelessness and faulty judgments.

But at this time and in all the periods there are a great number of men of whom in this book there is no memorial, without whom the *Telegraph* could never have grown to greatness—all those very able members of the editorial staff who hardly wrote a word except on someone else's copy or on proofs, who selected from the vast amount of material which flowed in every night what made the next day's issue and produced it in attractive and readable newspaper form. Nor was their contribution on news stories alone. How many of the signing stars would not admit under the truth drug how much their finished product owed to arrangement, heading and cross heading and, above all, however they may have fumed at the time, to the cutting by the ' sub '?

The early period is rather obscure but I could mention in the middle years E. P. Nuttall, Arthur Rowe, and several others, night-editors, chief sub-editors or sub-editors, and for the present day still more, for the work has become vastly more necessary and more complicated.

This is in no sense a roll of honour and there is no reader interest in giving a list of names of those of whom almost all one could say would be that they were really good sub-editors. Only a newspaperman would know that there is no higher praise.

CHAPTER IX

THE WINTER

VERY soon the claim of the greatest circulation in the world had to be brought down to the greatest circulation of any morning paper.

It is commonly said in Fleet Street to-day that the waning of the *Daily Telegraph* was due to the first Lord Burnham's failure to react to the competition of the *Daily Mail* from mistaken judgment as to its seriousness, from complacency, or from the indolence of old age.

There could have been no doubt whatever about the seriousness of the attack, but this argument assumes that the *Mail* was a plant of slow growth, which could have been stunted by the wind of fierce competition. The *Mail* at once had a circulation of 171,000, in two years it rose to 400,000 and in the next year to half a million. This was not the sort of thing which could be dealt with by a little tinkering of modernization.

It is true that the way to victory lies in attack, and even if you decide to rely on defence you cannot keep the enemy out of your trenches by sitting in your dug-out, however safe it may appear in the early stages of the offensive. It is equally true that you cannot turn elderly Home Guards into first-class assault troops against a tough and ruthless enemy. But if the military parallel is sound, the appreciation on which *Daily Telegraph* tactics were based should be clearly understood.

Much of the Fleet Street criticism is illuminated by

hindsight and based on an over-simplification of the problem.

Lord Burnham had a very important decision to take and he took it, rightly or wrongly, with his eyes open. He had to decide whether he would go chasing after the *Mail* in the field of circulation or whether he would establish a new position for the *Daily Telegraph* between the halfpenny Press and *The Times*, which then had a dwindling circulation and was far from invulnerable.

As a young man his reaction to competition was immediate, direct, and violent. In 1858 he at once increased his penny paper to eight pages in answer to the *Standard's* reduction to twopence. In 1896 he viewed the situation otherwise but the circumstances were different and his decision, if not the best one, was based on sound reasoning.

Harmsworth had called a new reading public into existence, as he and his father had forty years before. To compete for that public the *Telegraph* would have had to reduce its price. That it could well afford to do; and to the reader a halfpenny meant something in those days. But that in itself would not be enough. Lord Burnham could not make the *Telegraph* a halfpenny paper by halving its price. He would have had to do more than alter his make-up and import white space with a little brightening up and tightening up here and there. He would have had to make drastic changes in the editorial content and the approach to the news and problems of the day, and he was not minded to make them.

If to-day the *Daily Telegraph* were to come down to the price of the *Daily Express* and nothing more it would not get the *Daily Express* circulation. But if circulation is the be all and end all should not it mould itself on the *Express*? One powerful argument against this is that the result would be a bad newspaper, because *Daily Telegraph* proprietors and staff are not *Express*-minded and originals are always better than copies. There is no single pattern for a good newspaper, which is an excellent thing for the reading public.

The middle road at the end of the century looked very attractive. The numerical lead in readership might be lost but there remained a very substantial circulation wavering on either side of the quarter million. In classified advertising, which is less subject than display to the hazards of trade fluctuations, the *Daily Telegraph* held a unique position. 'Display' was good and soon Gordon Selfridge was to set a faster pace for the West End stores. From the two main sources revenue had never been higher. Only the timid might have felt cause for anxiety and Edward Lawson was not a timid man. There was no sign that the young lions who had grown long in the tooth were being replaced by less noble beasts. Sala was irreplaceable but Sala was also unchangeable and well might not have gone down so well in the twentieth century, Courtney did not roar so loud as those he replaced, but roaring had gone out of fashion, Beatty Kingston had gone but Dillon was at the height of his powers, the South African War was the chief news interest and Bennet Burleigh was still the greatest war correspondent of the day. J. B. Firth and later E. C. Bentley were writing leaders more simply than Arnold but with no less authority, knowledge, and force. Iwan Muller, though his time was short, had greater political wisdom and wider sources of information than anyone of the old days.

It is not possible to make a true comparison of the staff of the seventies and eighties and the staff of the nineteen-hundreds. The old days were the days of giants, but they were also the days of pigmies. Some of the old giants may have been of higher stature but there was certainly now a greater number of big men in the company. It was a good staff, missing perhaps some of the flamboyancy of twenty years before but writing with real merit and inspiring greater confidence in an influential and responsible section of the community. The surface of the middle road seemed good and the verges showed little signs of narrowing. Though it might have been better, the position was secure for fifteen years or more after Lord Burnham was supposed to have abandoned it.

It is easy now to see how many improvements could have been made without departing from the middle of the road policy. To one who remembers some of the men there is no doubt that Lord Burnham's loyalty to old friends in every section of the paper was some handicap to progress, but a claim that greater liveliness in Peterborough Court would materially have slowed the march of the *Mail* or that the *Telegraph* had in Lord Burnham's lifetime reached a point of difficult or no return cannot be justified. The winter came not from the success of the *Daily Mail* but from the failure of the *Daily Telegraph*, a failure due to deep-seated and structural causes which prevented its equipment to provide for a readership which still was there if anyone had had the imagination, the courage, and the drive to seek it.

If anyone doubts this they should study what happened when the change came. Lord Camrose did not go whoring after strange gods. He found recovery, not by chasing after the mass-circulation papers but by establishing a firm course along the middle road, guided by *Telegraph* tradition, which accorded with his own inclination. What could be so recovered could have been so maintained, but it was long after 1896 that the position was lost and the loss was not realized until it was too late to stage a counter-attack without a different commander.

Reflection on this story inspires the thought that this sort of movement may be inherent in the business and perhaps, as has been said of arts, newspapers ' like pro-jectiles describe their parabolas and fall '. Certainly it is difficult to find any long-established newspaper, dead or alive, whose progress has not shown this sort of graph. Some have suffered a drastic change of control or method and resumed the upward curve, some have been driven into the ground.

Some of to-day's most strident successes may not have been launched long enough to reach the downward curve, and this thought may be a comfort to puritans.

Whether all this is so or not, *Daily Telegraph* decline was not due to any inevitable and irresistible force. There is a bad patch in the record for which there should be no excuse, but for which there can be much under-standing.

Some improvements were made before the advent of the *Daily Mail*. The disappearance of the full page of three-decker leaders, which Garvin writing later about the *Telegraph* placed in 1896, had actually taken place some years before. A few more changes followed the arrival of the *Mail*. Paragraphing of the two- and three-column speeches and news stories appeared gradually and almost furtively, shortly to be followed by the occasional cross head. The chief points of speeches were made in an introduction, but generally there was little real sign of modernization.

In editorial as in advertising lay-out there is great virtue in the intelligent use of white space but there was scant appreciation of its worth in the columns of the *Daily Telegraph* which remained solidly packed with information.

Outside the paper, the crowded sixteen-line contents bills no longer tried to summarize the whole of the day's news in double-crown, but bills did not remain as short and as striking as Le Sage's own

DEATH OF
THE QUEEN

THE KING.

If Le Sage has a very big share of credit for the early success he, though much more his employer who kept him in his chair, cannot escape the responsibility for the failure to keep pace with progress in the years before the First World War.

He was too old to pull a weight far heavier than any which fell to him in the early years and of too jealous a disposition to share the burden. To William Gilliland who was appointed Assistant Editor he would hardly speak.

Letter writers of more modern view addressed correspondence to the Foreign Editor, the News Editor, or the Sporting Editor, to be answered with restrained fury by 'the only Editor of the *Daily Telegraph*'. Three times the second Lord Burnham appointed news editors, but Le Sage saw them all off by making their posts impossible. He would never use the telephone and to his last day in the office he gave the engagement to every reporter by his own hand. And that was June 30th, 1923, and he was eighty-six years old.

He was unquestionably in his time the greatest of the news craftsmen who play the most vital part in the building of a great newspaper. That his own passionate love of the *Telegraph* and its proprietors' regard and affection for him caused his staying on not only after he was past his best, but after he was past being good, was at once his tragedy and that of the *Daily Telegraph*.

The decision should have been taken at the top.

DAILY TELEGRAPH

Price One Penny.

THIS DAY'S NEWS.

Thursday Nov.ᵣ 26ᵗʰ

OFFICIAL TELEGRAMS from INDIA
Position of Havelock at Lucknow
Arrival of Reinforcements
Pursuit and Defeat of the Delhi Rebels
News of the Miscreant Nena Sahib
Dupin, the Political Renegade
Later Intelligence from America

The Monopolist Rogues in Gas
The Fraudulent Coachbuilders

DAILY TELEGRAPH

LARGEST CIRCULATION in the WORLD
With Extra Half Sheet.
Thursday. April 20th.

THREE DAYS LATER from AMERICA
Pursuit and Rout of Lee's Army
6 Confederate Generals, &c. Prisoners
Pres. Davis's Escape from Richmond
Full Details of Federal Victories
The Naval Attack on Mobile
WEST COAST OF AFRICA MAIL
Letters from France, Austria, Australia
The Russian Epidemic: Official Report
The Law Courts—First Day of Term
The Alleged Unity Bank Frauds
Newmarket Races: Hotspur, &c

DAILY TELEGRAPH

LARGEST CIRCULATION in the WORLD
SIXTEEN PAGES.
Wednesday, May 9.

SIEGE OF MAFEKING

MESSAGE from BADEN-POWELL
TO LORD ROBERTS

MASTER of the ROLLS RESIGNS

IMPORTANT LEGAL CHANGES

WITH THE YEOMANRY
AT THE FRONT

Daily Telegraph

BRITAIN
AT WAR WITH
GERMANY

CONTENTS BILLS
Above: 1857, 1865. *Below:* 1900, 1939.

Le Sage's devotion to the paper was too intense for anyone to expect him to suggest his own retirement, and it must have required plenty of devotion to face the burden at his age, for he never spared himself.

Wisdom can be found in unexpected places and for great men whose prime wish is to leave an undiminished reputation there is much sound sense in Lorelei's advice in *Gentlemen Prefer Blondes*, ' Leave them while you're looking good.'

When Le Sage retired it was perhaps inevitable that Fred Miller should succeed, as he had been doing much of the work for some time to enable Le Sage to complete his sixty years in Fleet Street. When Miller died in the next year Harry Lord Burnham played with the idea of bringing in a great editor, but decided not to go outside Peterborough Court and to content himself with appointing a very good one. With no reflection on anybody in the office at the time, it should have been abundantly clear that the editorial reorganization and modernization could only have been achieved by an outsider of great experience and authority who would see everything with a fresh eye.

It is true that Lord Camrose achieved the first and most important stage of recovery with the men appointed by Lord Burnham, but he had the fresh eye and possessed the outside editorial experience, the knowledge, and the drive which Lord Burnham could only have found in an imported Editor.

The time of Miller's death was full late for the necessary changes of policy because circulation, which had been some 230,000 before the war, had dropped to 180,000 by 1920 and was sinking rapidly.

That was the first opportunity missed and the second, about the same time and even more serious, was the replacement of machinery without change of size. The old unwieldy long page was a hopeless handicap to sales and one which no changes of typography and lay-out within the page could minimize. In a motor age you can only sell carriage horses to undertakers. And so a change which might have been gradual, had to be violent and the *Daily Telegraph* was sold by private treaty.

At the end of this chapter I interpolate out of its place in time a short note of the fusion with the *Morning Post* because it is the story of a like decline for not very dissimilar reasons but with a less happy ending.

In the Red Untrue Story Books, which seem to have formed much of the light reading matter of some of the inspirers of the Royal Commission on the Press, the bad barons of Fleet Street roam the countryside seeking whom they may devour.

In the sad story of the *Morning Post* the casting was quite different. The maiden was in distress, surely enough, but competition was the dragon and Lord Camrose was the knight-at-arms alone, for he had parted company with his brother and Lord Iliffe, but never palely loitering. As the rescuer he galloped, or more accurately cantered, to the cries of distress, not perhaps wholly altruistic, but after all even the knight-at-arms expected to get the girl, however honourably.

Discarding the imagery, the story can be simply told. Lord Camrose in the first instance had no knowledge of the matter whatever. Colonel Ivor Fraser, general manager of the *Morning Post*, told me that it was in financial straits and asked me to approach Lord Camrose to discover whether he would be interested in its purchase. I consulted Lord Camrose and he empowered me to continue discussions.

The *Morning Post*, a newspaper of long and honourable tradition, and fine purpose, was suffering a decline in some ways similar to that which we have described in the *Daily Telegraph*, the chief reason of which was that it persistently and resolutely maintained a policy of extreme conservatism which had little support in the country at large. The decline had gone further than that of the *Telegraph* because the circulation was lower, the plant had been disposed of (the paper being printed by contract with a general printing firm), and the editorial staff, though of the highest quality, had been cut far below what was essential for a national newspaper.

As in the case of the *Telegraph*, the only remedy was a blood transfusion and the financial resources of the company were inadequate to give it. They were not prepared, and indeed it might have been difficult, to seek fresh capital themselves and therefore took the only alternative of offering the paper for sale.

Lord Camrose's intention was not necessarily to cease separate publication, and indeed the *Morning Post* continued independently for months.

On consideration he decided that continuance was not a practical proposition. The *Morning Post* editorial staff had been numerically so depleted in the interests of economy as to be almost on a care and maintenance basis. To build up again would be a long and very expensive matter. He had his own very definite ideas of what a good newspaper should be, and the result would not have been sufficiently different from the *Daily Telegraph*.

There was a limited field for the circulation of what is generally described in Fleet Street as a ' quality ' newspaper, yet a field far larger than most newspapermen would have thought, as has been proved by the growth of the *Daily Telegraph* to a million circulation.

So the decision was taken to amalgamate. Almost all of the *Morning Post* staff were absorbed in the joint venture or found employment elsewhere. Lord Camrose's acceptance, after the transaction, of uncovenanted responsibility for pensioners of whose existence he was unaware gave a pleasant flavour to the end of a sad story of the loss of independent life of a great newspaper.

Morning Post readers as far as could be judged came over in a body to the *Telegraph*, and though perhaps they may have deplored the compulsory mellowing of their Toryism, were on the whole well satisfied.

Much could be said about the great tradition and record of the *Morning Post* but the purpose of this book is to tell the story of the *Daily Telegraph*, and their joint story only after the union.

Some of the principal posts on the editorial staff are to-day filled by *Morning Post* men who have brought with them much of the spirit of that great paper.

CHAPTER X

OTHER MATTERS AND OTHER MEN

IT is difficult to avoid an omnibus chapter in which to deal with events, subjects, and persons who do not naturally fall into the other sections. Those included here are not necessarily of any lesser importance in the story.

In this strange jumble, my first subject is sport. The proprietors were quick to sense the interest in racing and its possible development. Unlike writers on other sports, *Telegraph* racing correspondents have always been anonymous. In early issues Hotspur, Rough-scratcher, and Epaminondas appeared, but only Hotspur survived the passage of the years.

In the fifties racing was still chiefly the sport of the so-called upper class, and large crowds, except possibly for the Derby and St. Leger, were unknown. The part of Charles Greenwood as Hotspur in popularizing the Turf was comparable to that of Clement Scott for the theatre. Greenwood died in 1903 after twenty-five years' service. His opinions were quoted at Jockey Club meetings and he was looked up to by his colleagues of other papers as the greatest racing journalist. Whilst reading a race, he was always surrounded by a listening crowd of colleagues.

With the authority of a Lord George Bentinck but with the suavity of a Chesterfield, he would enunciate the history of the race in a few short, pregnant sentences, keeping his field glasses almost immovably upon the distant horses, and describing everything that occurred in the level accents of impartial justice and unswerving accuracy.

Greenwood was the first racing reporter whose work was as acceptable to the ordinary reader casually interested in racing as it was to the constant racegoer and the expert.

It has always been the aim of the *Telegraph* rather to write with understanding and knowledge of racing and the thoroughbred than to find the winner of the 2.30 and in the course of pursuing the first aim it has made no worse a job than its competitors of the other. Readers should reflect that if racing correspondents could predict the future with any certainty they would not be wasting their time in their arduous task of public information, for all the attractions of the best salaries which Fleet Street could offer.

When Greenwood died in 1903 he was succeeded by Sidney Galtrey who served both régimes until his death shortly before the Second World War. Galtrey was in the Greenwood tradition and was generally accepted as the leader of the racing journalists of his day.

In the early years of the twentieth century and until the First World War the *Daily Telegraph* made a feature of hunting reports, and their hunting correspondent was Harry Davenport at Melton Mowbray. Davenport had not himself hunted for years and was accustomed to collate his information on the newly popular device, the telephone. His chief difficulty was to find anyone in a fashionable Melton, Pytchley, or Warwickshire field who had the slightest idea of where they had been or what hounds had done. Lord Camrose revived the hunting reports between the wars, when the hunting correspondent was Captain Lionel Dawson, a distinguished naval officer and a nephew of Martin Ross, part-author of *The Experiences of an Irish R.M.*

For other sports and games the *Telegraph* has looked for knowledge of the game and ability to write about it rather than brilliance in its practice. Sometimes the two qualifications have been combined. Sir Pelham Warner and Douglas Jardine have in the past written on cricket, and on golf we have Leonard Crawley, in his day the best amateur player and, now that Bernard Darwin has left daily journalism, its best writer.

Wallis Myers, a scholar turned sports writer, was a first-if not top-class player and beyond question the greatest authority on lawn tennis at any time and in any country, who wrote with a graceful ease which made his work very attractive. In the 1914–18 war Wallis Myers was put to leader writing, in which task he showed versatility and force as well as his habitual elegance.

Wallis Myers also had a better news sense than some specialists. At a silversmith's where he was arranging for an inscription on one of his trophies he happened to notice an unfinished medal carrying the date of the Coronation in 1902, then unpublished, and was able to give the paper a scoop. Curiously enough by piecing together various conversations he was also able to give them the first information of the postponement. Myers died, before his time, in 1939 and lawn tennis has not yet found and perhaps never will find his equal.

Philip Trevor was never more than a competent club wicket keeper but he knew his limitations. At an Oval match early in the century the Gentlemen were short and Charlie Alcock asked Trevor to fill the vacancy. ' Thank you very much but I have too much sense ' was the answer.

But if not a great cricketer Trevor made the game interesting to *Telegraph* readers for very many years of what everybody over sixty considers to be the best years of English cricket. He combined with cricket rugby football, thus setting a precedent to two very eminent successors, Howard Marshall and E. W. Swanton.

Trevor's days were in every sense spacious and I still remember with horror an international match in Paris, when I had to deputise for him in the emergency of his sudden illness and found that I had to fill two columns with a game of football.

Sir Theodore Cook, later editor of the *Field*, was the first and as a writer the most distinguished of the rowing correspondents.

Perhaps it is the thought of Henley that turns the mind from rowing to fashion and the interests of women.

Women had done specialized work in newspapers before but probably the first of women reporters was Miss Billington of the *Daily Telegraph*. Billington, as she liked to be known, was a formidable figure, six foot high with a face more distinguished for its force of character than for beauty. She could, and occasionally did, write about dress and cosmetics, though she had little interest in the first and little use for the second. She preferred men's jobs and was largely used on the news side of matters of interest to women. She was particularly well liked by Queen Mary as Princess of Wales and later in her fatal illness Queen Mary constantly sent flowers to the nursing home. The acceptance of women on newspaper staffs in this century owes much to the sterling worth, experience, and good fellowship of Mary Billington.

What fashionable women wore in those times was in the *Daily Telegraph* the province of a much more feminine figure of the opposite sex, C. P. Little. A short, plump man, considerably overdressed, with a remarkable flair for remembering faces, Little was a well-known figure in the society of Edwardian days. He was either liked or detested by women of the new society according to whether he did or did not mention where they were seen and what they were wearing. Beginning as a small-part actor he followed this by-path of journalism in the *Daily Telegraph*, in another London morning paper, and for New York, and for a while had a great success socially and journalistically and enjoyed a considerable income.

Fashion in the *Telegraph* was developed and practised by the Hon. Mrs. Forester for many years until the formation of a woman's department covering all the interests of women and particularly fashion in a more modern way, with every assistance of the photographer and the artist.

For painting, the rough and tumble notices of Sala and other *ad hoc* art critics assigned, sometimes rather cynically, by Le Sage, gave way to work of real distinction with the employment of Sir Claude Phillips in 1896.

Claude Phillips was a distant relative of the family and a man of remarkable knowledge and taste who served the *Telegraph* for an altogether inadequate remuneration. He never complained about this but only threatened periodically to leave when the printer was unduly rude about his indecipherable copy. Claude's handwriting was execrable, his use of unfamiliar names and foreign words copious, and his corrections almost as voluminous as his original matter; these, and the fact that he always wrote on a number of small sheets which he sent in neither numbered nor in order, caused a certain amount of irritation in the composing room. Claude had in 1897, shortly after his joining the *Telegraph*, been appointed Keeper of the Wallace Collection where he recognized and rescued from the bathroom Titian's ' Perseus and Andromeda '. He was the first to appreciate the genius of Rodin and on his mantelpiece was always the signed and dedicated sketch in clay ' Despair '. Whilst Rembrandt was always his painter, he was no obscurantist champion of the classics and found affection for the work of Manet and Degas. He had been fortunate enough to be able to give years of his early life to travel and study, and art criticism could well do with more of his like to-day.

With Claude Phillips served an Edwardian figure who outlasted the Georges—A. C. R. Carter, art correspondent and critic, now in retirement. Carter had an encyclopaedic knowledge of the history of pictures in the sale room and his knowledge of art prices tended unfairly to discount his real merit as a judge of artistic values. For over fifty years, in addition to his work for the *Telegraph*, he was the editor of *The Year's Art*. Carter had a heavy-weight panache which admirably fitted him for the rôle of King Arthur's Champion at the banquets of the Knights of the Round Table, a task which he performed for many years. His sonorous voice and magnificent bearing made him a fine figure, despite an unforgettable suggestion of another knight immortalized by Tenniel. His old-world presence and vastly impressive white moustaches gave a stately grace to Peterborough Court and to Fleet Street and so did his work to the columns of the *Daily Telegraph*.

Music had special consideration from the *Telegraph* throughout its history. Joseph Bennett was the first musical critic and remained the principal one till 1906. In those days no one was encouraged to be too much of a specialist. Bennett had to cover the lying-in-state of Gladstone both at Hawarden and in Westminster Hall as well as his normal musical work. At the time, Bennett had as assistant Lionel Monckton, better known as a composer. Though he proved that his talent was for light opera, Monckton was a better news man than most critics. Hearing as he was passing the Adelphi of William Terriss' murder, he somehow got into the theatre and produced the best newspaper story of the day. Robin Legge succeeded Bennett with Herbert Hughes second, and musically more knowledgeable than either of them but of more restrained personality, F. Bonavia. After a few years with Hughes as chief came Richard Capell who might also qualify for inclusion in the war correspondents chapter. Despite being at the age at which colonels (fifty-five in a young man's war) were being retired for senility he served most gallantly and effectively in the Western Desert and in Greece. When I saw him with the Eighth Army they told me that they could not keep him out of the line.

In the theatre, though perforce some notices had occasionally to be written by others, all that mattered till the end of the century was Scott.

On Scott's resignation, Courtney did most of the dramatic criticism but as he was more used in other ways his share became less and that of Malcolm Watson greater. Watson was theatre correspondent and critic and editor of the regular feature, the Thursday theatre page, though nobody dared call anyone editor in Le Sage's hearing.

Then in the Courtney tradition came another scholar, but from Cambridge not Oxford—W. A. Darlington who has filled the post for thirty-five years with George Bishop succeeding, after an intermission, to the work of Malcolm Watson.

In literature, until the advent of W. L. Courtney, book reviewing was farmed out through Le Sage to suitable members of the staff. Courtney started the weekly book page and was succeeded by Arthur Waugh, the father of Alec and Evelyn. With Courtney commenced the practice, which continues to-day, of giving reviewing to distinguished contributors as well as to staff members. Now that we can follow the modern custom of having lots of editors on one paper at one time we can say that George Bishop is literary editor.

Inspired by the success of ' Paris Day by Day ', ' London Day by Day ' was started in 1888.   It never had the same success and for good reason.   Paris was written by men who knew their world for the eyes of those who did not and was therefore interesting, London by men of narrow social contacts for a public much better informed about the events and persons forming the subject of comment.   It was appreciated that the imitation fell short of the original, and Albert Vandam, the author of *The Diary of an Englishman in Paris*, who had a vast knowledge of Paris and little of London, was imported to brighten up the London feature.   It is no good importing a process unless you can find similar technicians to operate it.   ' London Day by Day ' became a long catalogue of personal and institutional happenings which were considered to be better placed there than in the news columns, with a very occasional clever paragraph of the true ' Diary ' type, gleaming like a diamond in a jet necklace.   It is only fair to those responsible to say that they suffered from the propensity of the proprietors to pull their punches on personalities, a grievous handicap to columnists.   The feature dragged on, died at the beginning of the First World War, and stayed dead until resuscitated in a different form by Lord Camrose.

' London Day by Day ', pseudonymously produced by my god-child Peterborough, is the work not of one man but of a team and readers would be surprised by the vast trouble which may have to be taken in the procurement, verification, and production of a short paragraph.

Hugo Wortham, once in a varied career a music critic, and a man of diverse and sometimes surprising knowledge, is the present Peterborough and for some years had William Deedes, the Member for Ashford, as his principal assistant.   Judgments are perhaps better passed by the reader, but I would say that the present ' London Day by Day ' is about as interesting as its predecessor was dull.

The *Daily Telegraph* was the pioneer of the modern type of crossword puzzle with the trick in the clues which require thought and knowledge. The crossword puzzle came from the U.S.A. but the clues of the early ones were only antonyms and synonyms.

The puzzle has been a vast success, and maliciously I like to think of the mental anguish there must have been in Printing House Square before they decided that, dignity or no dignity, the damned thing was too popular, and they must follow the *Telegraph*.

I must include in my round-up as well as features a number of individuals not necessarily of less distinction than those mentioned elsewhere, but less easy to classify.

My first is Walter Bell, the historian of Old London. Bell came with the *Sunday Telegraph* in the South African War. The *Sunday Telegraph* deserves a short digression. On isolated occasions the *Telegraph* had produced a special edition on Sunday when the news warranted. On April 9th, 1899, appeared the first number of a regular *Sunday Telegraph*, and seven weeks later the last. The public outcry against a seven-day paper was terrific. That the staff did not have to work seven days and could be rested on another day did not seem to occur to anyone. Alfred Harmsworth came out with a *Sunday Mail* in competition.

However difficult it may be to understand in these days of what are known as dual offices, there was no doubt of the strength of public feeling. Lord Rosebery, who was not prone to the exaggeration of issues, appealed for a ' Truce of God '. Whatever view may have been taken by the Almighty, on May 20th there was a truce of practical expediency and the *Sunday Telegraph* disappeared.

Bell's knowledge of old London was very great and

he wrote about it attractively in the *Telegraph* as well as in books. He was no one-track specialist but an all-round journalist of high order with a fund of special knowledge of many subjects on which he wrote with style and sincerity. Everything about him was thoroughly genuine except his preposterously unconvincing wig. I owe him a debt of gratitude for the use of material which he had compiled for an unpublished history of the *Daily Telegraph*.

Willie Wilde, Oscar's brother, was for a time on the editorial staff. If his vices were less unusual than his brother's so too was his talent, but he was not without a certain eccentricity. Legend has it that he used to work in the sub-editors' room stripped to the waist, a practice considered very much more peculiar then than it would be to-day. Untidy in mind and dress, he had a large straggling moustache and was known in the days of Colonel Cody as Wuffalo Will. He wrote some brilliant sketches of the proceedings of the Parnell commission and had a certain ability, but he was unreliable and did not last long.

Not only at home did the *Daily Telegraph* search for talent. In 1910 Luigi Barzini, with a great reputation in Italy as a descriptive writer, reported the first international aviation meeting at Bournemouth, at which C. S. Rolls was killed. Barzini brought back some of the floridness of Sala and was much used for special and war reporting. Before the First World War a young man called André Géraud worked in the *Telegraph* building as correspondent of the *Echo de Paris*. Later, as Pertinax, he established a reputation as one of the greatest political journalists of Europe and was a regular contributor to the *Telegraph*, and has since the Second World War resumed his writing in its columns.

Joseph Hall Richardson is referred to elsewhere but should have longer mention.

A good deal of management and organization is required and for this, though there were many brilliant minds in the office after J. M. Levy's death, there was no tidy mind till Hall Richardson took over the care of these matters. Though intensely jealous of almost everybody in the office, curiously enough he was prepared to fill in all the gaps without directly or indirectly seeking any credit for himself. Richardson was engaged by Le Sage immediately after his return from Disraeli's funeral and served for nearly fifty years. To him is due almost all the credit of the many successful *Daily Telegraph* funds.

His grey beard and precise manner gave the impression of his being more old-fashioned than he really was. Though he lacked a very vivid imagination, he had plenty of enterprise. It is difficult to see how the set-up of the first twenty years of this century could have worked without him, and it was perhaps a misfortune that his ability made an unsound structure appear temporarily safe.

John Moss I include because he was a character, and as an example of special industry even in the days when nearly all eyes were more on the job than on the clock. I remember him in the time very shortly before he passed from history into legend.

A sports sub-editor, single-handed he did all that to-day is done by a numerous staff. Certainly the work is now greater and more complicated but there was a lot of truth in what John Moss used periodically to say as he thumped his table, ' Every night here I do the work of six men.' Of how many hours his nightly shift consisted there is no record. He used to get his sleep at his desk waiting for copy. There were members of the staff who remembered seeing him go home, but very few, and like so many men who work that way he resented the suggestion of any assistance. He preferred to grumble and continue his six-man job.

I should like to recall to the old-timers amongst the distributors of newspapers the figure of Frank Dawe, the first and for a long time the only *Telegraph* circulation traveller, and possibly the first of all circulation travellers. With his flowing white beard he must have appeared more like a visitant from the lower slopes of Mount Carmel than from those of Ludgate Hill. He had many of the qualities of the graduates of the school of the prophets including a fine capacity for invective.

He served the *Telegraph* loyally and fervently for some thirty years, retiring after the First World War. He would hear of no rival paper and I am sure that he did his rounds on foot in the morning when all the bus-horses appeared with white rugs advertising the *Tribune*. Dawe breathed and dreamed *Telegraph*. How he must have bored the 'reps' in the Travellers Rest above when the news came up of the first million sale.

There is another *Daily Telegraph* character I would like to recall to old-timers on the editorial side of Fleet Street. John Martin was brought to London by Le Sage from his old paper the *Western Morning News*. He served the *Telegraph* for some fifty years, the last twenty-five in the Lobby and Gallery of both Houses of Parliament.

With his mutton-chop whiskers, always neatly dressed in a black suit, and with an old-world courtesy and dignity he remained a Victorian figure in the Edwardian and Georgian ages. There are always two ways of getting news, and the one to be recommended if you want to come again is by being thoroughly liked and trusted. John Martin did much to establish the credit of the profession at a time when journalists were still rather suspect by politicians and Government departments hesitant about releasing information.

He lived to make recommendations in 1919, at Lord Salisbury's request, for the improvement of reporting in the House of Lords. Martin suggested, and Lord Salisbury, Lord Curzon, and Lord Selborne were prepared to accept, that there should be two rows of seats for reporters on the floor of the House behind the Official Reporter. There were serious objections and nothing came of it.

Martin continued with the *Daily Telegraph* for some years after his work as lobby correspondent had been undertaken by W. J. Foss. Very active and always well informed, Foss succeeded in maintaining the confidence of ministers and men of all parties. I can only remember one occasion when he caused embarrassment to the paper.

In Ramsay Macdonald's premiership in 1929 the *Daily Telegraph* announced that the Government had taken a decision to arrest Gandhi. It can hardly have been thought that this information would cause any evasion of the course of justice as for some time Gandhi had been challenging and expecting arrest.

However, one morning in my room I got a telephone call from Arthur Watson, the Editor, asking me to come down to his room. There I was introduced to a police inspector and a sergeant who had come down to demand the source of our information of what they alleged to be a State secret. In accordance with accepted newspaper practice, we politely refused and the inspector left. Later in the day Watson was ' invited ' to call on Tindal Atkinson, the Director of Public Prosecutions, whom he was unable to assist.

After the police officers had left I said to Watson, ' As a matter of interest where did it come from?' and he told me that Foss had been able to get it perfectly properly in the course of his work on certain information given him by J. R. Clynes. We then decided that through unofficial channels we should indicate to the Home Secretary, Clynes, that he had better call off his sleuths, and we heard no more of the matter. These happenings were reported to the Newspaper Proprietors' Association and the upshot was that an undertaking was given by the Government that proceedings of this kind under the Official Secrets Act would in future only be taken on the fiat of the Attorney-General. As far as I know this still holds.

One member of the staff should be mentioned not so much for his part in the *Daily Telegraph* as for his subsequent distinction—Charles Bowerman. Bowerman was a ' stab ' hand in the composing room of the *Daily Telegraph*, a member of the London Society of Compositors, and of His Majesty's Privy Council, proud of all three distinctions and a great English craftsman and gentleman.

Charlie Bowerman once told me that he first saw me in a perambulator at a wayzgoose at my uncle's house at Taplow, and many things besides which I have found useful in this book. I will only record directly some composing-room views of the copy of the stars. Sala's handwriting was influenced by his early training as a wood engraver and he won the prize. Claude Phillips got the wooden spoon, *nemine contradicente*. Scott wrote so small that he could get on a sheet of notepaper enough to fill a column. T.P. had the peculiar habit of typing his copy without spaces and stops and afterwards dividing his words and sentences with strokes of the pen. Kipling was no favourite because of his tiresome habit of insisting on having returned to him any galley proof which carried a correction in his own hand.

A great newspaper owes much to its production staff and I should like to pick out for mention more of those who

> ' maintain the state of the world
> and their desire is in the work of their craft '

but space is limited and the task of selection too difficult.

Labour in the newspaper industry is more highly organized than in any other, and the traditions of the trades unions of longer standing are more firmly fixed than those of almost all others. Some dozen unions cover the work with strict and sometimes complicated lines of demarcation. Generally speaking, they are very conservative, in the best sense of the word, but have an approach to labour questions that can only be understood by those who work with them.

This can be illustrated by a story of the General Strike in 1926. Incidentally, the *Daily Telegraph's* strike story is one of good improvisation but not of great glory. With overseers and others working we could have produced a full-size four-page paper in Peterborough Court but when Winston Churchill came down to the office with his plans for the *British Gazette* he was promised all available labour. So the *Daily Telegraph* for the first few days published tabloid editions printed in a number of non-union jobbing shops and distributed by an emergency organization with commendable efficiency. Before the end of the strike work was resumed in Peterborough Court. One night Robertson, the stereotypers' overseer, a thorough trades unionist, obviously and deliberately strike breaking, was standing in the foundry after all the plates for the night's edition had been cast. I was carrying plates to the presses. A life-long member of the Stereotypers' Society, he had hardened his heart to work with non-unionists, but he could not cross the line of another union, and Robertson said to me, ' I wish I could help you with that but it's a Natsopa job.'

The pickets were only concerned with preventing operative members taking part in the work in accordance with the principle of the solidarity of organized labour, but were delighted to see the paper getting out. If you think on that and on the mentality behind Robertson's remark you will understand something about the printing trades unions.

Whatever the shortage of space I must give full mention to the greatest newspaper master-printer who ever trod Fleet Street. No old *Telegraph* man can think of the *Daily Telegraph* without recalling the great figure of Francis Caine, for forty years head printer of the paper. Adequate tribute to a head printer can only be paid by those who have worked with him on the stone, and I know that I could find no words of praise for Caine that would not be heartily endorsed by every night editor and sub-editor who ever worked with him. No one outside the profession can realize the responsibility and the trial of temper and energy involved in getting a large newspaper to bed, particularly if that newspaper is full of classified advertising, much of which is just as late matter as the greater part of the news. Caine carried through the introduction of the linotype machines in the nineties and lived to print a forty-page *Daily Telegraph* in the years before the Second World War. Whatever the strain and stress, he and Arthur Watson, the Editor, never lost their heads or their tempers. Caine's great broad-shouldered figure, massive bat-eared head, and measured movement through the room, in themselves inspired confidence. One of the begetters of the complicated piece wage scale of the London Society of Compositors, he claimed to have outlasted all head printers who really understood it.

Caine came to the *Telegraph* on loan from the Linotype Company when the machines were first introduced in the nineties and spent a year at the *Daily Mail* before returning permanently to the *Telegraph*. In that time he once turned Lord Northcliffe out of his own composing room because it was the printer's not the proprietor's responsibility to see the paper away. That shows something of Caine's character.

IT TAKES COURAGE AS WELL AS SKILL TO DO A CROSSWORD PUZZLE IN THE PUBLIC LIBRARY.

This cartoon by H. M. Bateman is reproduced by kind permission of the Proprietors of *Punch*

Lord Curzon with Field-Marshal Lord Roberts, V.C., at the Mutiny Veterans' party
at the Albert Hall, June 23rd, 1907

Caine felt the transfer of ownership as keenly as any
of the family, for whom he had a deep affection. He was
fortunate in being able to find a like regard for his new
master, not because he was a man of fickle loyalty but
because he found his new proprietor like his first, a
thoroughly competent tradesman and a warm-hearted
human being. Caine carried through all Lord Camrose's
big technical changes and retired a happy man because
he had seen his loved paper re-established, and because
he knew from the way in which he had been treated
that his share in the work was fully appreciated.

Alphabetically in newspaper life advertising comes first
unless you feel compelled to include accountancy; in
this chapter it comes last.

Obviously, an important part in the growth of the
Daily Telegraph was played by the advertisement department. The public to-day probably know enough
of newspaper economics to realize that the revenue from
sales hardly begins to pay for the news service which
they enjoy. In varying degree that was always true.

The development of advertising revenue is shown by
the comparison of something under ten shillings for the
first day to £8,784 in a thirty-two page paper on a day in
May in 1939 before the outbreak of the Second World
War. That development could not have taken place
without the efforts of many very able and energetic
advertising men. It would be a poor compliment to
their achievement to list them with the soulless brevity
which the Bible gives to the Kings of Israel and of Judah.
I will only mention two of their number, one of the old
and one of the new dispensation. In the middle years
the *Telegraph* did not have to bother much about soliciting
advertising, it was more a matter of sitting and waiting
for it to come in. H. Meek, for many years advertisement manager, was not so well named as might seem
from his appearance in the photograph group on Lord

Burnham's eightieth birthday, but even in his young days he was not much of a go-getter and Rowland Lee was the principal canvasser for a long time before he became advertisement manager in 1912. For some twenty years after the turn of the century he was one of the best-known characters in Fleet Street. ' Rowley ' did himself supremely well, even for those days when more advertising business was done in the bar than in the office. But however good a day he had had both for business and refreshment, on his return to the office in the late afternoon he would send for his inside man and without a note give him the dates of insertion and full particulars of every order that he had taken, without a mistake. And the only engagement I ever knew him late for was his funeral.

Calculations of rate per inch per thousand, market research, and all other complications of the modern advertising agent were to him unknown, but he was in his day a first-class advertising man. He brought back one day a contract for £50,000 from Barkers, a vast sum at that time, without any sign of having accomplished anything out of the way.

For the greater part of his working life he travelled about his daily avocations by dog-cart in a top hat which he wore with scant dignity and great reluctance.

When he died in 1922, however much he had outlived his time he was a hard man to replace.

The only adequate replacement would have been a well-staffed, modern, stream-lined advertising department headed by a man of equal individuality and more instructed talent, but even at that late hour *Daily Telegraph* management had not grown up so far towards modern requirement.

That had to wait until Sir Gomer Berry put in G. P. Simon, now General Manager, as advertisement manager with a well-organized department. Simon had knowledge not only of newspaper work, which is largely salesmanship, but also, through his experience at the London Press Exchange, of the technical side of advertising. He gathered round him a highly competent team and set them to work with such success that by the beginning of the Second World War the *Telegraph* was publishing an average of twenty-eight pages a day throughout the year and occasionally as many as forty pages a day, justified by a high and varied news content and supported, not only by classified advertising, in which the *Telegraph* had always been supreme, but by attractive and incidentally pleasingly remunerative West End and general display advertising of the highest quality. The advertisement revenue of the first *Daily Telegraph* was seven shillings and tenpence, and on one day in the spring of its centenary £17,041.

CHAPTER XI

FEATURES, FUNDS, AND FÊTES

ALMOST from the commencement the proprietors decided to take an interest in discovery of all kinds. In 1872, at Arnold's suggestion, they placed a thousand guineas at the disposal of the trustees of the British Museum to send George Smith to Nineveh, and the expedition brought back fragments which completed the story of the Flood.

So much of Henry Morton Stanley's work appeared in the *Daily Telegraph* in the seventies that he must have very special mention.

Brought up in a workhouse, butcher-boy, haberdasher's assistant, cabin boy, a soldier on one side in the American Civil War and a sailor on the other, Stanley's reputation was well made before he came to the *Telegraph*. Representing the *New York Herald* he had found Livingstone, and whether Livingstone was lost or merely mislaid was a matter for Stanley to argue out in the Press and on the platform with Sir Henry Rawlinson and the Royal Geographical Society.

Le Sage met Stanley at Marseilles on his return from Ujiji and, encouraged by Le Sage's deceptive stolidity, Stanley was so indiscreetly expansive that his employer, Gordon Bennett, wired ' Stop talking '. The friendship formed at this meeting brought Stanley to see Edward Lawson in Fleet Street and led to the great 1874 expedition across the continent of Africa. Gordon Bennett, who had a contract with Stanley and with a big man's generosity had no rancour about Marseilles, agreed to share the cost and left all the organization to the *Daily Telegraph*.

From then on Stanley was a constant contributor to the *Daily Telegraph* in his five years with the Association Internationale du Congo and in his strange adventure to relieve a German scientist turned satrap, Emin Pasha, Gordon's Governor of the Equatorial Provinces. For months Emin was unwilling to gratify the urge of a London Committee for his rescue, until his troops revolted and he had to agree that he was a suitable subject for salvation.

Stanley was something of a soldier of fortune but he was a soldier of the fortune of Africa and if the purpose of exploration goes beyond ethnological and geographical discovery to making unknown and savage lands live in the minds of men and creating the interest which leads to their civilization, Stanley was amongst the truly great explorers.

The *Daily Telegraph* gave Stanley the largest newspaper circulation of the time in this or any other country. Stanley's articles did more than give Victorian readers thrilling stories of adventure; they had a considerable part in the inspiration of the nineteenth- and early twentieth-century development of Africa.

Some ten years later the *Daily Telegraph* largely financed Sir Harry Johnston's exploration of the Mountains of the Moon. In this venture Johnston was the first to explore Kilimanjaro. In 1899 the *Telegraph* supported Lionel Decle's journey from the Cape to Cairo.

The *Telegraph* provided the greater part of the support for the 1933 and 1936 expeditions to Everest on which so much was discovered that helped the final conquest of the mountain. With valuable co-operation from Indian Army Signals, the communications made a record and set a standard for rapidity and efficiency.

The *Daily Telegraph* was the first newspaper to organize functions on occasions of national importance. The first and the greatest was for the Jubilee of Queen Victoria in 1887. Thirty thousand children were entertained in Hyde Park and reviewed by the Queen. The Duke of Wellington once said that it would test the capacity of a general to march an army into Hyde Park. The *Telegraph* managed it somehow and marched them out again, everyone having been fed and carrying a cup as a souvenir of the occasion. The organizers of newspaper shows to-day could still learn something from the Victorians.

This was the greatest function organized by the *Daily Telegraph*, but I have little doubt about what was the most dramatic. In 1907, fifty years after the Indian Mutiny, Lord Burnham decided to give at the Albert Hall a Christmas dinner and party to the veterans. Perceval Landon undertook the management.

The scene was set, the boxes and galleries were crowded, and in the arena sat down over six hundred of the gallant survivors. In the chair was Field-Marshal Lord Roberts, a Mutiny veteran and V.C. Lord Curzon made one of the greatest speeches of his life, Lewis Waller with his fine presence and golden voice declaimed Rudyard Kipling's tribute to

> the remnants of that desperate host
> that cleansed our East with steel.

And then came a thrill which, though only a boy of seventeen at the time, I will never forget and which moved that vast audience immeasurably.

Faintly in the distance came the skirl of the pipes, ' The Campbells are coming ', the air that first told the beleaguered of Lucknow that relief was close, growing slowly in volume as the pipers drew near, and in they swept led by Piper Angus Gibson of the Black Watch, the last survivor of those who played in Colin Campbell's men on the great day of 1857.

In its hundred years' life the *Daily Telegraph* has organized some forty funds of different kinds and varying importance. The first was in 1862 in the Lancashire cotton famine caused by the American Civil War. It produced over £6,000, a very considerable result for a newspaper fund in those days. Nearly the same amount resulted from a very different appeal, the shilling fund for Dr. W. G. Grace.

Letters poured in from every section of the community and I will only quote from the letter sent to my grandfather with his subscription by the Prime Minister, Lord Salisbury.

> I beg to enclose a centenary of shillings to use the current phrase. I have not touched a cricket ball for more than 50 years—so I am afraid that I can only claim a 'locus standi' as owner of a village cricket ground. You are kind enough to refer to the cricket of my sons. I regret to say that it is wholly despicable.

I trust that Lord Cecil and Lord Quickswood will raise no objection to the unauthorized publication of this parental comment.

The first really big-scale fund was the widows' and orphans' fund in the South African War, which provided the then unheard of total of £255,275. The First World War saw the Belgian Relief Fund of £151,707 and King George's Fund for Sailors £231,209. The *Daily Telegraph* was always ready to open its columns for a good cause. Prominent of the lesser efforts were the Titanic Relief Fund, the Scott Memorial, the Sulgrave Manor appeal for the preservation of the family home of George Washington, and the Nurse Cavell Memorial Fund, which erected in St. Martin's Place the Frampton statue which, whatever its artistic merit, shows the versatility of the sculptor of Peter Pan. The unveiling of this memorial was the last public function of Queen Alexandra. When the ceremony had ended, walking away with Lord Burnham after a few gracious observations about the occasion, she told him that if the *Daily Telegraph* were to promote any more like it he would have to buy a new frockcoat, which was unquestionably and lamentably true.

The earlier funds were known as shilling funds and their success was due to the large number of comparatively small subscriptions received from readers of the paper and was evidence of the strength of *Daily Telegraph* circulation.

Two funds after the First World War, the Boy Scout Appeal in 1921 of £78,780 and the Shakespeare Memorial Theatre Fund in 1926 of £276,000, owed more to extraneous stimulation.

In particular, a very large sum for Stratford was given by subscribers in the United States and the fund owed much to the energy and organizing ability of Percy Bullen, *Daily Telegraph* correspondent in New York.

The greater difficulty in raising money was only partly due to the diminished circulation of the paper at that time. The day of the successful newspaper fund, dependent only on appeal through the columns of the paper, was over, except possibly where there might be a very specially dramatic and urgent appeal. Though people are still very generous they no longer read a newspaper article and reach for their cheque book or go out to buy a postal order. At any rate many fewer do. The raising of money for good causes has become a very specialized and expert business and newspaper support at the best can be only subsidiary.

For various purposes the *Daily Telegraph* organized a great number of special theatrical and musical performances, the most notable probably in Lord Camrose's régime. From a long list I will only mention the matinées for Sir Henry Irving's centenary attended by Queen Mary, and Dame Marie Tempest's jubilee in the theatre attended by King George and Queen Mary, a very remarkable week of performances of *Pilgrim's Progress* at Drury Lane, and in music the most successful series of Henry Wood Memorial Concerts.

The Antiques Exhibition at Olympia in 1920 was a great artistic and popular success. Its promotion was a gallant and creditable endeavour with certainty of considerable financial loss. This loss was calculated, and understandable if it is realized that the whole of Olympia had to be decorated and provision made for the transport and display of exhibits with an insurance value of over six million pounds.

Throughout the hundred years, at intervals parties of notable people were held to see the wheels go round. The first in June, 1884, was for the opening of the new office which for many years was, with its Pillar Hall, a feature of Fleet Street until in 1929 it was replaced by a building of greater capacity and more austere magnificence. A company of some six hundred included the Prince of Wales, his brother the Duke of Albany, Lord Houghton, Serjeant Ballantine, John L. Toole, Henry Irving, Squire Bancroft, and many ambassadors and leading figures in literature, law, science, and society. Amongst the members of the Services was Colonel Fred Burnaby, who talked at the party to Bennet Burleigh, destined a few years later to describe his heroic death in action. In July, 1896, a reception was held of seven hundred guests including the Duke of Cambridge, Prince Christian, and Prince Charles of Denmark. The party inspected the installation of thirty linotype machines, the first battery to operate in any London newspaper office.

With other items of more technical interest and more difficult to understand they were told that it took less than four minutes to print a ton of *Daily Telegraphs* and that 144 tons of newsprint specially manufactured at the *Daily Telegraph's* own mills at Dartford were used weekly.

King George V and Queen Mary visited the office as Prince and Princess of Wales.

Entering the composing room the Princess said, ' Now I am going to see my favourite paper printed.' The Prince in a voice which could be heard all over the room said, ' I read *The Times* but I suppose that is because I was brought up on it. The Princess reads the *Telegraph* and tells me what is in it.'

In 1930 Edward Prince of Wales dined with Lord Camrose in the present building with a party of some forty guests and afterwards made a most thorough study of the night's production.

Other parties were too numerous to mention. A very memorable and, it would seem, a not very fruitful one was a visit of German editors a few months before the outbreak of the First World War.

Returning from by-products and side shows to the paper itself, it is interesting to observe how its contents of matters other than news was continually changing. At the beginning, additional interest was found in special signed articles by members of the staff, usually hung on a special peg but sometimes only demonstrations of the virtuosity of the writer. In the early middle age of the paper articles of this type became rarer, to make space for the concentration of special interest news and features, the Woman's Page, the Theatre Page, the Music Page, the Book Page, and smaller space features as gardening, dogs, stamps, and so on.

Cycling was an early special interest to get space, sometimes given with an ulterior motive such as a proposal to found in the East End a club ' to combine cycling and the spread of Unionist doctrines '.

In June, 1895, is recorded the wedding at Ashtead, Surrey, of what must have been the original Daisy. ' Along the merry party sped, the happy couple leading on a tandem, with the bride on the front saddle . . . attired in a fawn-coloured cycling costume, knicker-bockers included . . . her coiffure, from which streamed a white veil, was garlanded with orange blossoms . . . a most elegant, tasteful, and up-to-date affair.'

Soon, also, space had to be found for serial publications, which became more and more prevalent. In the First World War space was restricted, though not so sharply as in 1939–45. Nevertheless, the *Daily Telegraph* had many notable special features of which perhaps the most distinguished were Rudyard Kipling's *Fringes of the Fleet*, *The New Army*, and *France at War*.

The immediate post-war period stepped up the *Telegraph* practice of serial publications of books of importance. American diplomats were first in the field with their pre-war and early wartime experiences, James Gerard from Berlin and Brand Whitlock from Brussels. The Services had their share in Sir John French's diary, Admiral Sir Roger Keyes's *War Memories and Naval Adventures*, General Sir Hubert Gough's *Fifth Army* book, and, the best seller of them all, Admiral Gordon Campbell's *My Mystery Ships*.

It seemed difficult at the time to get away from war but place was found for Nellie Melba's *Memories and Melodies* and André Maurois's *Life of Benjamin Disraeli*.

A return to war came with a fine book, Lawrence's *Revolt in the Desert*, a shorter version of the *Seven Pillars of Wisdom*, which gave temporary relief to a harassed circulation manager. Occasional attractions of this kind can always put the paper into fresh hands because of the opportunities they give for an advertising campaign, but the paper will not stay there unless it satisfies the day in and day out needs of the reader. It is like a drug and the addicts need continual and increased doses. What a good newspaper needs is the normal stimulants of news enterprise, attractive presentation, and sound opinion.

The selective mentions here give little idea of the great number of good and interesting serial publications, but catalogues make poor reading.

It is indeed remarkable that the *Daily Telegraph* published the memoirs of the two premiers of the first war, Asquith and Lloyd George, and Winston Churchill's history of the Second World War.

It is now Lord Camrose's policy, except in special cases as that of Winston Churchill, to avoid long series in order that the leader page articles can be more closely related to the news of the day. The *Daily Telegraph* is essentially a newspaper for men and women who want news and is not unduly loaded with features designed for those who prefer diversion to information of the world's happenings.

One of the problems of the early days seems to have been to continue reader interest in the so-called silly season. Topics were not unusually silly in the months of August and September, nor for that matter were readers, but it is difficult to-day when there is always the cold war to hot up interest to realize quite how dead things became at the end of July when the contents of newspapers were mainly political and there was no autumn session and the long vacation of the courts was both long and real.

Therefore the last twenty years of the century saw the appearance of the correspondence features, usually coming in with the grouse and going out with the pheasant. They were the stand-by of the time when politicians went into winter quarters, and there were no apparent signs of official life.

Some of them were slight and short: ' The Age of Love ' followed by a titleless series on the continuance of engagements when affection is dead, ' Are Appearances Worth Keeping Up? ', ' The Slavery of Drink ', a forestalling of Gaylord Hauser, ' The Art of Losing Fat ', and the first threat of Bikinis. ' I have told bathers who desire to wander about amongst ladies of superior station with no covering but a clout that they are not of the class of people that Broadstairs desires to entertain ' wrote the Pier Commissioner in a powerful epistle opening up the correspondence.

But some were of deeper purpose and more enduring appearance. The first big subject was ' Is Marriage a Failure? ' in 1888. Le Sage ran this, starting with a letter by Mona Caird, the authoress. Letters poured in like a tide, from first to last over 27,000. When interest began to fade, Le Sage called Europe into existence to redress the balance of Britain and sent the Paris correspondent to interview Zola and Dumas Fils.

This produced neither high thought nor good copy. Zola said, ' This question of marriage does not interest me much ' and Dumas gave less definite and longer-winded advice than *Punch*, ' Let those who want to get married do so, and let those who do not care for marriage abstain from it.'

The Vienna correspondent, on the other hand, wrote that the controversy ' is exciting considerably more interest in Eastern Europe than the Bulgarian question '. I fear it would be futile to hot it up now as an antidote to the cold war.

' Do We Believe? ' was an even greater success.

Ordinary unorganized correspondence from readers was for a long time spread about the paper and therefore lost importance. Its concentration is of comparatively recent practice and has added considerably to its interest. Topics tend to persist but they are spontaneously generated and naturally maintained. *The Times* noted with concern the growth in importance and authority of *Daily Telegraph* letters to the Editor and at one time gently hinted to some of their letter writers that if they wrote to other papers they could not rely on the continued hospitality of the columns of *The Times*. This did not produce any noticeable effect on the *Daily Telegraph*.

Though we may be still a little shy on bishops, V.I.P.'s equally well qualified to express opinions on the things of this world are in good supply. The *Telegraph* problem with letters to the Editor is not to maintain their number and importance but the obvious one of selection from a very large post bag.

Letters to the Editor, that is to say letters of reasonable length, not of three or four lines, are one of the main distinctions of a so-called 'quality' newspaper. The practice of giving them has a double merit, in that they are both an attraction to the reader and an opportunity for the airing of views differing from or contrary to those of the paper itself. That this opportunity should not be confined to papers with a limited circulation but should still be available in a paper with over a million sale must be in the public interest.

CHAPTER XII

CLARIONS AND DRUMS

TWO events in this history deserve a chapter to themselves. I group them together because they are both concerned with Germany and in both of them the *Daily Telegraph* made a sensation, incurred criticism, and in some quarters inspired dislike.

The first is the famous Kaiser interview in 1908. So many stories have been given piecemeal of its provenance that it is surely time to tell the whole history.

I am particularly confident in stating these facts because whereas many of my sources of other information have been second hand, in this case I have been told the story by every one of the principals except the Kaiser—by Harry Lord Burnham, by General Stuart-Wortley, and by J. B. Firth. They all agree and a triple coincidence is held by detectives to establish a certainty.

At the suggestion of King Edward VII, who thought it would be a good thing for the Kaiser to have a closer knowledge of England, General (then Colonel) Edward Stuart-Wortley placed Highcliffe Castle at the Emperor's disposal for several weeks in the summer of 1907. The General, though housed elsewhere, remained in attendance on the Kaiser and had many long discussions with him on Anglo-German relations.

During the visit, Major-General Brocklehurst, later Lord Ranksborough and then equerry to Queen Alexandra, wrote to Stuart-Wortley asking him to approach the Kaiser with a request for an interview with W. T. Stead for the *Pall Mall Gazette*. The Kaiser refused, saying that he neither liked the man nor the paper, but the idea of a newspaper interview remained with Stuart-Wortley. The next year Stuart-Wortley was the Kaiser's guest at the German manœuvres and had further conversations. Towards the end of the visit he asked permission to set down something of the substance of their talks with a view to publication in a newspaper. The Kaiser agreed subject to the finished script being submitted to himself and to von Bülow.

Stuart-Wortley took his notes to Harry Lawson at the *Daily Telegraph*, who had them written into the form of an interview by J. B. Firth. Firth agreed the manuscript with Stuart-Wortley and it was sent to the Kaiser.

The Kaiser in his own words ' carefully examined it ' and wrote to Stuart-Wortley. ' It embodies correctly all the principal items of our conversations during the recent manœuvres, and deals in a most reasonable and straightforward manner with the justified complaints that I have to make against certain organs of the English Press.'

He did not sign but made three slight verbal alterations and sent it on to von Bülow with instructions to suggest any desirable alterations in the margin.

Thereafter it is hard to determine the truth through the clouds of excuses. Von Bülow who was on holiday claimed that he did not read it, but sent it to Berlin marked ' confidential ' and ' revise carefully '. The Under-Secretary in his turn claimed not to have read it, but to have passed it to a Councillor, and so it came back to the Kaiser and from him through Stuart-Wortley to the *Daily Telegraph* and was published.

One of the German official excuses was that the importance of the document was not realized at the German Foreign Office because the manuscript was ' in illegible

LORD BURNHAM (LOQ.):—"WHAT, MAKE THE TELEGRAPH TWO-A-PENNY!
PERISH THE THOUGHT!"

Reaction to the *Daily Mail*

MOONSHINE.—Sept. 29, 1894.

THE CENTURIES OF GRACE.

Sir E. Lawson. "DON'T MENTION IT, DOCTOR, AND THANK YOU FOR WHAT YOU HAVE DONE FOR MY CIRCULATION."

Sir Edward Lawson presenting the testimonial cheque to Dr. W. G. Grace

handwriting on poor, thin paper '. In fact, it was 1,500 words of double spaced typescript on the office's best paper (of most impressive thickness and importance, with wide margins for correction), and in any case it was sent to the officials with a covering note from their Emperor and therefore should have earned more than a casual scrutiny.

Prince Metternich, the Ambassador in London, who might have given the Kaiser useful advice, was not consulted at any point and was left to say ' now we may shut up shop ' as he read his *Daily Telegraph* of October 28th, 1908.

Probably the German officials were mainly influenced by the source of the manuscript. The Kaiser can never have been the easiest author to sub-edit, still less to ' spike '. Certainly the Kaiser was under no illusion and indeed was very pleased with the whole business until he saw the British and German reaction to the publication. He liked the idea of an emotional appeal made directly to the people of another country over the heads of their Ministers. It was theatrical, and so by nature was he.

You English are mad, mad, mad as March Hares. What has come over you that you are so completely given over to suspicions quite unworthy of a great nation? What more can I do than I have done?

I have declared with all the emphasis at my command in my speech at Guildhall that my heart is set upon peace, and that it is one of my dearest wishes to live on the best terms with England. Have I ever been false to my word? Falsehood and prevarication are alien to my nature. . . .

I have said time after time that I am a friend of England, and your Press, or at any rate a considerable portion of it, bids the people of England to refuse my proffered hand, insinuates that the other holds a dagger. How can I convince a nation against its will? . . .

I resent your refusal to accept my pledged word that I am the friend of England. I strove without ceasing to improve relations, and you retort that I am your arch-enemy. You make it very hard for me. Why is it?

He turned back to the Boer War and recalled that when France and Holland had fêted the Boer delegation which came to seek European intervention, he had refused to receive them.

So far so good, but then came the passages which gave offence in England and proved that the man whom Baron von Stumm called ' le plus grand gaffeur de l'Europe ' could not open his mouth without putting his foot in it.

Just at the time of your Black Week, in December 1899, when disasters followed one another in rapid succession, I received a letter from Queen Victoria, my revered grand-mother, written in sorrow and affliction, and bearing mani-fest traces of the anxieties which were praying on her mind and health. I at once returned a sympathetic reply. Nay I did more . . . I worked out what I considered to be the best plan of campaign under the circumstances, and submitted it to my General Staff for their criticism. Then I despatched it to England, and that document likewise is among the State Papers at Windsor Castle, awaiting the serenely impartial verdict of history.

Even after eight years the memory of the humiliation of the early part of the campaign was too keen to make agreeable any talk of the offer, however well intentioned, of advice from a distinguished foreign amateur. It might at another time have been thought friendly if tactless. In 1908 it caused apoplexy in the Service clubs and rage in the four-ale bar.

The interview went on to justify the creation of a strong German army and to give warning to England of the Yellow Peril, which however sound a prophecy was not calculated to give unmitigated pleasure to our new allies, the Japanese.

The rage caused by the South African references set the tune of the reception of the interview in England, and it was easy to find the argument that the whole purpose was to lull the suspicions of England and give time for the German ship-building programme.

That would have been attributing to the Kaiser a subtlety which he never possessed. Certainly it was no deep laid scheme of German statesmen, because the reception in Germany was far worse than in England and the Kaiser's advisers did their utmost to disown him. Von Bülow even went so far as to deny that the famous plan had ever been considered by the German General Staff or sent to England.

In Germany, the Kaiser was roundly accused of allowing his personal feelings and family sympathies to override the interests of the nation. And so the interview could not have failed more signally in its purpose. The first half of it maddened Germany, the second half enraged England.

In retrospect it would appear that as far as the Kaiser was concerned it was a well-intentioned project of blundering stupidity. It is more interesting to consider why the *Daily Telegraph* published it. It could be said that once having invited the interview it would be improper suppression not to publish, but the *Telegraph* did not plead that. It did not feel called upon at the time to relate the circumstances of the interview or to justify its action. Some time after von Bülow's death in 1930, and after the *Telegraph* had passed from his control, Viscount Burnham told the story, and on his decision to publish said that he believed that the interview ' might—and in the opinion of those concerned would—make for world peace and better understanding amid the lowering clouds that already darkened the European outlook '. He realized the risk but took the view that it could not do harm, and might do good.

Looked at purely as newspaper enterprise it was a remarkable achievement, coming our way like so many newspaper coups not by planning but by the chance of personal contacts.

Another personal contact involved the *Daily Telegraph* in the most stormy episode of its history, the publication in November, 1917, of the Lansdowne letter, miscalled the Peace Letter. Lord Lansdowne had been Foreign Secretary, 1900–05, and was Minister without Portfolio, 1915–16.

The middle of a war is never a time for dispassionate examination of the respective merits of stated war aims and unconditional surrender. What the effect would have been on the next thirty years of European history if the First World War had ended earlier and differently may be a good subject for speculation to-day. Then the violence of Lansdowne's opponents altogether outweighed the moderately phrased support of those who agreed with him.

Quotations from the letter will show that it did not deserve the two most popular epithets ' craven ' and ' inept ' though the third, ' inopportune ', may have been justified.

Lord Lansdowne wrote:

> We are now in the fourth year of the most dreadful war the world has known, a war in which, as Sir W. Robertson has recently informed us, the killed alone can be counted by the million, while the total number of men engaged amounts to nearly twenty-four millions.
>
> Ministers continue to tell us that they scan the horizon in vain for the prospect of a lasting peace, and without a lasting peace the task we have set ourselves will remain unaccomplished.

And later: ' We are not going to lose this war, but its prolongation will spell ruin for the civilized world, and an infinite addition to the load of human suffering.'

Briefly, Lord Lansdowne's points were that stimulus would be given to the peace parties in the enemy countries if it were made clear that we did not contemplate the destruction of Germany as a Great Power; that we did not propose to impose on her a government not of her own choice; that, except as a legitimate war measure, there was no intention of excluding Germany from the great international communities; that we were prepared to examine in concert with other Powers the questions connected with the freedom of the seas; and that we were also prepared to enter into a pact for the settlement of international disputes without having recourse to war.

As far as Lansdowne himself was concerned the accusation that the letter was due to sudden loss of nerve cannot be justified. In 1916 he had submitted a memorandum to the Cabinet in almost identical terms, but in all the controversy and against all abuse his regard for Cabinet tradition prevented his making any reference to it.

He had on November 22nd submitted his main points in a letter to Mr. Balfour, Foreign Secretary, though without stating specifically by what method he would make them public. His first intention was by question in the House of Lords. Balfour in somewhat vague terms expressed agreement with all of them, but his reply of November 22nd began, ' I do not know that this is a very suitable time for discussing peace matters, I rather think not '. One could hardly describe that as very decisive. Balfour, owing to his absence in Paris, was unable to see the finished letter but asked Lansdowne to submit it to Lord Hardinge ' who has my complete confidence and knows my ideas '. Lord Hardinge had no objection to the draft.

Lord Lansdowne had more definite support from other leaders. Lord Burnham's memorandum of his conversation with him in the library of the House of

Lords shows that a week before the publication Lord Lansdowne, Lord Curzon, Balfour's successor as Foreign Secretary, Lord Loreburn, ex-Lord Chancellor, and Colonel House, adviser to President Wilson, dined together. The letter was read and discussed. All agreed that it was desirable that it should be published. Lord Curzon wished to make some amendments to the text which would not have altered the general purport. This was no hasty scribble of a panic-striken old man. Lord Lansdowne then showed the letter to Geoffrey Dawson with a view to publication in *The Times*, but Dawson refused to publish it. Lord Lansdowne then approached Lord Burnham in the library of the House of Lords, and after a long discussion Lord Burnham agreed and the letter appeared in the *Daily Telegraph* of November 29th. It was not splashed in any way but had a simple headline ' Co-ordination of Allies' war aims—letter from Lord Lansdowne '.

The Press reception was mixed, the violence of *The Times* under the direction of Lord Northcliffe quite unmixed, the abuse of Lansdowne going beyond relevant matters to attack his record as an Irish landlord. The newspapers controlled by Lord Rothermere and Sir Edward Hulton were equally violent, but the *Daily News* and *Star* in London and in the provinces the *Manchester Guardian*, *Yorkshire Post*, *Birmingham Post*, *Sheffield Independent*, *Edinburgh Evening News*, and others supported the letter. About a fortnight after the publication the *Saturday Review* summed up, ' Now that the malice of the Press and clubs is exhausted, we take leave to say that the publication of Lord Lansdowne's letter has done good '.

Lord Burnham was not surprised at his mixed Press, for he had not expected anything else from Press, politician, or public. The decision to face unpopularity for himself and the paper was a courageous one, taken because he believed the expression of such opinions from a leading statesman outside the Government to be in the national interest, and that a man of Lord Lansdowne's position should not be denied newspaper space for his views, particularly as they appeared to have the approval of the Foreign Office. If Lord Lansdowne had been refused by the *Daily Telegraph* he would have reverted to his original intention to raise the matter in the House of Lords.

Presumably newspapers would then have published much of his speech whether they thought his views harmful or not.

From my conversations with Lord Burnham in later years—I was in the Judaean Hills at the time and did not see him till after the end of the war—I do not gather that he was mainly influenced by his view of Lord Lansdowne's proposals—though he was generally in accord with Lord Lansdowne's policy. He felt that the opinion was worth stating and that Lord Lansdowne had the right to state it. He never thought that it could do harm, and on reflection later he thought that Bonar Law was chiefly concerned that it might be considered to be a Government-inspired *ballon d'essai*. But he had no doubt that purely from the point of view of *Telegraph* self-interest there could be no advantage.

Lord Burnham was disturbed by a speech of Bonar Law's to the National Conservative Union in which he spoke of the publication of the letter as a national calamity. Whatever his view of war policy or of Press exclusion of important opinion he was not prepared to accept a charge of inducing national disaster and on December 2nd he went to see Bonar Law. On his return to the office he dictated a note of the conversation of which I make extracts.

Bonar Law then came in, and said Lloyd George was very tired after a rough passage, and that he had not mentioned to him what I had said on the telephone because his difficulties with him were very great; that Lloyd George did not think much of Balfour, and the only result of telling him what I had said would have been that Hardinge would have been dismissed in the morning, and then Balfour might have gone too.

I said that I was sorry but that I was going to tell Lloyd George, and he said it was quite right that I should.

I told him the exact facts as set down in my memorandum of my conversation with Lord Lansdowne in the library of the House of Lords on Thursday last. Bonar Law thought that there had been some muddle, because, as Balfour had not seen the letter, he had not anticipated what it would be like. [Lord Burnham was presumably unaware of Lansdowne's letter to Balfour of November 22nd, which would have strengthened his case as Balfour could not plead ignorance of Lansdowne's views.] I said ' That does not alter the fact that he had specially asked Lord Lansdowne to submit it to Lord Hardinge, who had his complete confidence, and knew his idea.' He said ' No, that is so, but I can imagine myself in the same position.' I put it that we had to face the facts, and that on the general grounds of co-ordinating our war aims and revising our war policy, Lord Lansdowne's letter could not do much harm. He said that he differed from me, as they had telegrams from all the neutral countries saying that it had done harm.

He further said that he never thought of blaming the paper for the publication of the letter. He did not even know that it was not etiquette for papers to refuse letters from men of Lord Lansdowne's standing on the ground of disagreement with the views expressed.

On the exact words ' national calamity ' Lord Burnham records that he, Bonar Law, ' disputed with me as to whether he did not qualify the statement, but could not find a verbatim report of his speech. I said he did use those words. He said he did not mean them to apply to the newspaper publication.'

Then I said ' On Monday you may have a debate on the letter in the House of Commons.' He said ' Not if I can help it.' I said ' It may be forced on you. If so, and the question of the *Daily Telegraph* is raised, I expect you to say what you have just told me.' He said ' I should have said it in any case. I did not refer in any way to the paper in regard to publication. I was thinking of the letter. I imagined that Lord Lansdowne was big enough and responsible enough to take care of himself—to stand on his own record.'

And so the interview ended and Lord Burnham went next door to see Lloyd George, but he had left for the country.

Bonar Law said that harm had been done abroad. There is little evidence of that in the foreign Press. In France, *Echo de Paris* and *Figaro* ignored it altogether and very few papers gave it at any length. *Le Temps* supported Lansdowne and *L'Intransigeant* approved his suggestions in general but differed in detail. The Italian papers said nothing and the United States hardly noticed it.

Lord Esher wrote from Paris to Lord Lansdowne, ' Will you let me send a word of affectionate admiration for your courage and patriotic attempt to make our unfortunate people use their brains.'

In the next few months opinion came round to Lord Lansdowne's viewpoint. President Wilson made his peace proposals, and in a speech in February Lloyd George accepted the necessity of a restatement of war aims. After the Allied Conference at Versailles in the same month Count Hertling in a speech suggested an intimate meeting of the belligerent nations and generally was inclined to accept Wilson's terms.

Lord Lansdowne on March 5th had a second letter in the *Telegraph* based on Hertling's speech which met fairly general approval and brought no abuse for the paper.

Of the first letter I would conclude by saying that the wisdom of Lord Lansdowne's statement of views at that particular time may still be controversial; the propriety of a newspaper not refusing its columns to a statesman of such standing with such approval can hardly be disputed. The decision, right or wrong, was in accord with policy which did then, and I believe does now, govern the conduct of the *Daily Telegraph*, that we should put first what we believe to be the public interest without regard to any repercussion on the circulation of the paper.

CHAPTER XIII

MANAGEMENT AND CONTROL

IN its hundred years the *Daily Telegraph* has had six Editors—Thornton Hunt, Edwin Arnold, Sir John Le Sage, Fred Miller, Arthur Watson, and Colin Coote.

But until after the First World War the Editor's function was very different from what it is in newspaper offices to-day or even from what it was in most newspaper offices in the late nineteenth century.

Thornton Hunt probably and Edwin Arnold certainly were more writers than editors. The Dictionary of National Biography is not more precise than to say that Thornton Hunt ' practically edited ' the paper. Edward Lawson in his evidence in the Labouchere libel case describes Arnold as ' the head of my staff ' but he does not call him Editor. Le Sage, he says, was ' manager of the news department, having charge of the editorial correspondence, and generally assisting the Editor '.

Two of Le Sage's leader writers survive—E. C. Bentley and Sir Archibald Hurd. In the absence of Lord Burnham or Harry Lawson they had their subjects assigned to them by Le Sage but I doubt whether they ever had a strong guidance from him as to what they should write. The real Editor for the first fifty years was Edward Lawson, and after him his son Harry took much more direct and practical editorial control than any modern proprietor or chairman with the exception of their successor, Lord Camrose.

Peterborough Court was not in those days a great place for clear definition of function. Until two years before Lord Camrose took over there never was a news editor operating as such and the first general manager was appointed by him. In the earliest days the organization was departmentalized under the general control of the principal proprietor. As with the provincial governors in the Roman Empire, from time to time one or other of the more forceful departmental heads usurped greater power and responsibility. At one time some of the functions of a general manager were taken by Frank Hare whose real province was the paper mill.

In living memory the largest managerial responsibility was exercised by J. Hall Richardson who had been a highly competent reporter. He had charge of the managerial side of the editorial department. He also exercised a vague control over the mechanical departments engaged in production and was the first *Daily Telegraph* representative on the Council of the Newspaper Proprietors' Association. But Hall Richardson had no concern in the advertisement or circulation departments and no part in the financial organization of the paper. He was a man of experience, good judgment, and ability but of an awkward temperament. At intervals he and Le Sage were not on speaking terms although for part of the day they sat in the same room, a situation which imposed a somewhat heavy burden on their secretarial assistants in the task of interpretership and liaison.

From this account it may well be wondered how the paper attained and for many years maintained its astonishing success. It is easier to understand if one realizes how much the control of a successful newspaper is a one-man job. I can think of no case of a newspaper rising to success which had not behind it the drive and inspiration of a single personality, and this the *Daily*

Telegraph had in full measure. Edward Lawson was a trained printer and a natural journalist of the highest order. Walking with Max Pemberton down Fleet Street, Northcliffe pointed to the *Daily Telegraph* building and said to him, ' There's an old man sitting up there who can teach us all our business.' Northcliffe had a high and sincere regard and very considerable affection for his predecessor in popular journalism, though reasonably and properly he never pulled his punches in trying to break the paper which published his first contribution to daily journalism, an article on cricket.

Indeed, Edward Lord Burnham had great qualities as a newspaperman. In technical production his knowledge did not go far beyond the composing room, where after leaving the City of London School he served his apprenticeship, acquiring proficiency and speed sufficient to decide him, because of the higher earnings, to go on piece rather than on time. At the other end of the scale W. L. Courtney records that

. . . to see him at his best in his work as editor in his office—one should have watched him deal with a ' leader '. He would go over it line by line, word by word, making erasions here, adding a sentence there, deleting, strengthening, building up—and all the time explaining why he did this or that and what object he was aiming at. Whenever some important issue was impending he was at his post, alert, prompt in suggestion, quick in judgment, decisive in the conclusion to which he had arrived. Nine times out of ten Sir Edward was right; indeed to disagree with him through some obstinacy of one's own was generally to have to confess to a humiliating mistake.

The devotion of the *Daily Telegraph* to art, music, and the theatre was largely due to him. His interest in the theatre was special and his knowledge considerable. He married the daughter of an actor-manager, Benjamin

163

Webster, and Irving, John Hare, Bancroft, and many leaders of the stage were his close friends.

Politically he was more interested in men than in measures and the fact that for some thirty years his son was on the other side hardly gave him a moment's anxiety. He was a fine judge of men, both in his choice of staff and in his treatment and direction of them in their daily work. He was generally known in the office as ' the Guv'nor ' and Thornton Hunt writes to him as ' beloved master '.

He was intensely human and possessed in very full measure that invaluable quality in a newspaperman of knowing what interested ordinary men and women. He had a quick mind, abounding courage in editorial decision, and last but by no means least a magnificent sense of humour, and all this with great knowledge and experience acquired in the hard way. The real capital which he put into the enterprise was not the five hundred pounds of his eighth share but his qualities of brain and heart.

The *Daily Telegraph* may have shown a fairly untidy blueprint of newspaper organization judged by modern, or indeed by any standards, but it worked. The rooms may have been a bit short of labels on the doors but their occupants knew pretty well what they had got to do and very clearly to whom they had to look for guidance and control. They had a leader.

It was in no spirit of empty compliment that the staff deputation to Lord Burnham on his eightieth birthday described themselves as his family of Peterborough Court. He was the first to acknowledge the debt he owed to his father and never forgot that he was only twenty-two years old when their venture started and how much the soundness of the foundation owed to the more experienced craftsman. Though J. M. Levy's obituary notices pay higher tribute to his shrewdness

than to his intellect, large newspaper circulations are
not rapidly built by shrewdness alone.

When he died, at a time when all regarded his son
as the man behind the *Telegraph*, *Punch* did not forget
the share of the old man in that fantastic success.

> A name that all will link with the Cheap Press
> He seized the moment and he snatched success.
> The Proletariat pence he found would build
> A fortune for the shrewd and the strong willed,
> As well and swiftly as patrician pounds.
> Keenness that measures, kindness that abounds,
> Are not the worst equipment for the strife
> Of loves and interests that men call life.
> With him 'tis o'er, and many known to fame
> Have left less good and less enduring name.

At the end of the century Lord Burnham began
gradually to draw in from the office and more plans were
made and more leaders and special articles read over the
private telephone to Hall Barn. Pioneer in so many
newspaper enterprises, he preceded Lord Beaverbrook
in direction by remote control.

And gradually his son began to take greater responsibility. Harry Lawson had been brought up literally
and metaphorically in a different school. His mother
had never wanted him to go in for newspaper work.
She saw in him a future Prime Minister, as indeed he
might have been if he had devoted himself solely to
politics.

In most of his working life he could only be a part-
time newspaperman. For seventeen years he was a
member of the House of Commons and for some years
of the London County Council. He travelled abroad
extensively and in the First World War commanded
a reserve regiment of yeomanry.

Though in his father's lifetime the share which he
took in the management and control of the paper

became progressively greater, in the late eighties and nineties his position was complicated because he remained a Liberal until the South African War and was therefore out of sympathy with the politics of the paper. His change of view coincided with the break-up of the Edward Lawson-Arnold-Le Sage triumvirate through the failing sight and ill-health of Arnold.

With sound judgment, scholarship, and a deeper knowledge of public affairs than his father ever possessed, he had not the same training, experience, and flair as his father and his contribution to the news side of the paper was therefore less.

On the other hand, he was much more politically minded and better informed politically than his father had ever been, and in days when domestic and foreign affairs were infinitely more complicated and important. His father's only close friend in the political hierarchy of his time was Gladstone and the two men were destined to drift apart. In the first quarter of the twentieth century Harry Lawson was on terms of close personal friendship with Asquith and Lloyd George whose Premierships covered the greater part of the period, though except in war time he was their political opponent, and he knew well and was trusted by all the leading men on both sides of the House. Frequently they came to him for guidance and assistance and not only in matters connected with the Press. The result was that as the director of opinion in the paper he was one of the best, if not the best, informed men in the country. This and his breadth of view, knowledge, tolerance, and wisdom added immensely to the strength and authority of the leading articles. He was a man of wide culture and interests and under his guidance the attention given to the arts continued to preserve for the *Daily Telegraph* its distinctive quality.

But he had a share of the *défauts de ses qualités*. In his

private and public associations one of the most friendly, democratic, unpompous, and intensely human of men, in his direction of the news columns of his paper he somehow lacked the common touch. Though far from being a dull man, he was a most serious citizen. His affections were largely political, he was deeply interested in education, he took part in activities of many kinds for social betterment in this country and beyond its shores, and charitable work, not only that connected with his trade or profession, had his interest and his advocacy on the platform, in the banquet hall, and in the columns of the paper. In the words of a friend, ' he lighted candles in dark rooms '. Walter Runciman called him ' an unofficial servant of the Empire '.

He sincerely thought that a very large section of the public were concerned with the same worthwhile interests as himself and his views of what a newspaper should contain would have received universal approbation by the Royal Commission on the Press.

And this last is not a cynical observation. Anybody involved in the management of a newspaper is fully aware, and if it is a serious newspaper distressed, at the concern of good men and women about the fine causes for which little or no space can be found and for the worthy events which have to be left out, and even more for some of the others which have to go in. But however high your purpose in a newspaper, it fails if you cannot sell your copies, and, like public speakers, newspapers cannot afford to bore their public, nor must they omit or suppress what is of genuine public interest.

The result was that the *Daily Telegraph* in the immediate post-war period, despite much editorial improvement after Le Sages' retirement, seemed solid and dull, except to the few, and its general columns judged by news interest alone suffered from a Gresham's Law.

Nor was the heaviness of the news relieved by the

advertising. Varied and well displayed advertising, particularly fashion advertising, can be an attraction to the reader but the *Daily Telegraph* did not get this aid to circulation in sufficient measure. Classified advertising is far from negligible as a circulation builder and the *Daily Telegraph* never lost its hold on classified advertising, but ' smalls ' do not provide any enhanced attraction to the make-up. With a falling circulation there was a corresponding fall in store and other display advertising and Lord Burnham, instead of concentrating on its recovery, decided to call a new field into existence to redress the balance of the old and to get pages and groups of pages devoted to special industries. The majority of these industries were ' heavy ' and their publicity of slight general appeal. Judged by revenue alone this recourse was extremely successful but the make-up of the paper became awkward and unattractive to the reader, the intervention of three or four pages of advertising between news pages making for difficult reading. The paper looked solider and solider every day and of diminishing interest to women, who, after all, represent over half the population of the country.

And so, though the advertising gap was plugged, circulation continued to fall until by 1927 it had dropped just below the hundred thousand. Lord Northcliffe was reputed to have said that the paper suffered from nothing but Anno Domini. But the circulation trouble was not hardened arteries but anaemia, and could be and was remedied by blood transfusion.

The decision to sell, the reasons for which are explained in other pages, was for Lord Burnham a desperately sad one. Having been very close to him at the time I know how he felt. His first consideration far outweighing all others was the future life and success of the *Daily Telegraph*, secondly the interests of the now numerous ' absentee landlords ' in his family who depended upon its profits for their income, and lastly and hardly at all the conservation of his own fortune. Though he was not inclined by temperament to take risks he would cheerfully have taken them to re-establish the paper, if the risks had been entirely his own.

Though he only lived another six years, it was long enough to see the *Daily Telegraph* well advanced on the road back, and, like the big man he was, he found profound pleasure and satisfaction in the achievement of his successor and the progress of the newspaper which he loved.

Viscount Burnham's conduct of the *Daily Telegraph*, though immensely creditable, was not marked by commercial success. His very great talent was purely editorial and his business sense was the least well developed of his faculties. He was not tough enough for the fierce competition which started with the birth of the *Daily Mail* and was intensified in the first twenty years of the century. The management of any successful business in a highly competitive field requires beside the greater qualities of knowledge, judgment, energy, and enterprise some degree of cunning, which can well be possessed without unscrupulousness, and perhaps a soupçon of wholesome doubt of the complete trustworthiness of one's fellow men. Harry Lawson was absent when cunning was served out, and he found extreme difficulty in thinking ill of anyone.

Though he saw smaller circulation and diminishing revenue, his editorial conduct of the paper was impeccable and in accord with the best tradition of the *Daily Telegraph* and the highest standards attained by any newspaper at any time.

Lord Beaverbrook in 1917 wrote:

> We are aware of the merits of the *Daily Telegraph* in London. It occupies a position in the Metropolitan Press parallel to that which the *Manchester Guardian* claims

rightly enough in the North. If the *Manchester Guardian* get a readier recognition abroad it is due to the brilliant independence of its editorial attitude. The countervailing quality of the *Daily Telegraph* is its sure and steady interpretation of the movements of opinion among the innumerable middle class and upper class people of Great Britain. Speculation would be foreign to Lord Burnham's rôle in life. He is one who upholds the Pillars of Church, State, and Society; and the *Daily Telegraph* is purely conservative. This quality is as valuable to the nation as the trenchant radicalism of the *Manchester Guardian*.

And he concludes by rating Lord Burnham second to Scott as the greatest working journalist of the day.

That was the opinion of a rival, but for all the high standing of the *Daily Telegraph* and for all its wise guidance by Viscount Burnham its prospect of continued independent existence after the end of the First World War was far from reassuring.

CHAPTER XIV

FINANCE

AT this stage it is desirable to make some study of *Daily Telegraph* finance. No reader need be frightened away from these pages by thinking that it will contain analyses of balance sheets or a lot of figures of any kind. But it is interesting and important to this history to consider how a newspaper can have passed from desperate financial struggle through a period of great prosperity to decline and near fall.

Some financial details of the earlier and leaner years have been mentioned in an earlier chapter. The picture of the first proprietors, painted by some of their early opponents, showing them as business men intent on money-making with little concern for the news and literary side is entirely wrong. J. M. Levy was a shrewd man, though nothing approaching to a business genius, and though he kept a close eye on administrative expenses, he spent money freely on the content of the paper. His son Edward was in fact a very poor business man. When Hurdell, the cashier, or his successor Wentworth, brought him a balance sheet he would say, ' Take the damned thing away, my boy, I don't understand anything about it.' He was gratified and often surprised at their financial success, but I have failed to find that he did anything constructive to achieve it, except to make every effort to produce a good and readable newspaper. Only an obstinate popularity carried the paper through its haphazard methods of management.

It was not until the publication of the *Daily Mail* in 1896 and its growth and that of some other halfpenny newspapers that the *Telegraph* discovered the weaknesses in the structure which had stood well the competition of the nineteenth century. Circulation began to shrink, advertising revenue became more difficult to maintain, and production costs began to increase and it was not geared to stand the strain.

At the time of the sale to Lord Camrose it was generally believed that the *Daily Telegraph* was being run at a loss and was in serious financial straits, but this is completely inaccurate. In the whole of its history the *Daily Telegraph* never made a loss. Even in the nineteen-twenties though the profits had considerably receded from those of the good times of the past the *Telegraph* was never in the red.

Always the beneficiaries of the trusts were more concerned with income than a sound financial structure and there was never adequate provision for renewal of plant and development. From the beginning, the partners who played an active rôle had a minority holding. Lionel Lawson held a half and never took any part at all in the affairs of the paper. J. M. Levy and his son held between them three-eights. After J. M. Levy and Lionel Lawson's deaths their shares were divided amongst a very numerous family. Then Edward Lord Burnham held the largest single share ever held, but still less than half, and at the time of the sale to Lord Camrose Viscount Burnham, though generally considered the owner, never described himself as anything but the principal proprietor and his actual holding through all the trusts was not greatly over a quarter.

The continual policy of giving as much as possible to the beneficiaries did credit to the family feeling of those who exercised control, but showed very little business sense.

For very many years, irrespective of real profits, a fixed division of £124,000 was regularly paid; anything there might be over was used or accumulated for renewals or development or to make up the dividend in years when it had not been earned. One of the results was that by the end of the First World War the rotary machines were slow, antiquated, and incapable of good printing and, difficult as it may be for newspapermen who read this to credit, still driven by steam power.

Viscount Burnham was lucky at this time that the large wartime profits of his paper mill had placed in his hands a reserve for this large operation of replacement of plant. Unfortunately he rejected all advice to change the size of the page to what is known as the standard size. The old page-size with a three-inch longer column made a paper difficult to handle and, however made up typographically, old-fashioned looking and awkward to read.

It must be said that his decision was not solely due to obstinate conservatism but was influenced by the considerably increased cost if the change were not made gradually. Obviously if the size is to be changed the old machines must go on until the new can take the whole of the print. Apart from expense, double the floor space is required and the difficulties are considerable, but they were in no way insurmountable and it was subsequently done.

It became obvious that the paper was losing ground and that apart from changes in content and method a further large capital expenditure was required. The machinery installed in 1922 would have to be replaced. The part of the premises used for mechanical production was large, situated on an island between the narrow courts and passages at the back of Fleet Street. It was joined to the editorial offices by a bridge and constructed as a factory incapable of any other use except through a vast scheme of rebuilding.

The editorial section, though fully adequate for the work of the eighties, was altogether too restricted for the greatly increased staff essential in a modern newspaper. Accommodation for managerial staff was virtually non-existent and the advertisement department had for some time at great inconvenience operated in leased premises further down Fleet Street. Further, it was clear that a large sum would have to be set aside for development and promotion. Like the grasshopper, they had sung in the summer and ' *dansez maintenant* ' was cold comfort.

Viscount Burnham as principal proprietor owned about a quarter of the paper. He was the only proprietor to take any interest in the paper except for what he or she got out of it. Unless he were able to provide considerable finance on his own responsibility, for which his resources independent of the *Daily Telegraph* were not adequate, there seemed only two courses— to turn the partnership into a public company or to sell.

He considered the first. He had a circulation which had fallen to 90,000 and a reduced though still substantial yearly profit, not a really attractive proposition to take to the public, and he had a strong objection to acting as chairman of a company with responsibility to public shareholders where he had ruled with the unquestioning support of his unconsulted partners. ' Like Alexander he had reigned and he would reign alone.'

But that was a personal prejudice and he took the decision to sell on mature consideration because he was convinced, and rightly, that the sale would be in the best interests of the partners. He then had this difficulty to face. He wanted to make the best financial arrangement for the partners, most of whom were members of his own family, but he was deeply proud of the *Daily Telegraph* and determined it should only go to persons whom he felt certain would make a success of it and maintain its high tradition. As the only member of the staff whom he consulted at this time, I know that he had decided that unless he could interest Lord Camrose, then Sir William Berry, he would make a resolute attempt to solve his financial difficulties in other ways.

Lord Camrose was then Editor-in-Chief of the *Sunday Times* and Lord Burnham had watched the progress of that paper and of its chief with keen interest and had formed a very high opinion of the Berry brothers. Camrose was the man he wanted. It is probably equally true that the *Daily Telegraph* was the paper Camrose wanted. Certainly no transaction of this magnitude could ever have gone so smoothly. It was in the full meaning of the phrase a gentlemen's agreement.

Whether Lord Camrose and his brother Lord Kemsley and Lord Iliffe, who joined him in the purchase, paid the right price is sometimes a matter of reflection by the author. Judged by the present prosperity of the *Daily Telegraph* it might have appeared reasonably cheap, but it was a very fair and proper price taking into account the very large sums which Lord Camrose had to spend, which he did freely and fearlessly, for the capital improvements which were immediately required to enable the paper to hold its own in the fierce competition of Fleet Street. So came about the change of dynasty. The story presents a peculiar contrast to the intrigues and excursions which beset a similar change in *The Times* of 1908.

Most members of the staff regarded the change with suspicion and some personal anxiety. We did not know Sir William Berry, Mr. Gomer Berry, or Sir Edward Iliffe. Even the most apprehensive had to admit that the worst they could find said about them was to suggest that they were financiers, which curiously enough in a highly industrialized country is considered a term of reproach. Naturally they would be new brooms and it would be idle to pretend that some of the departments had not more than a fair share of cobwebs. There were some, with the highest affection for the paper and its principal proprietor, who not only realized that things could not go on as they were but even from pride in the paper saw good in the opportunity of development. That was a thought which it was indecent to express and which even its holders could not reconcile with their feelings for Lord Burnham and the great old paper.

When the transaction had been completed I asked Sir William Berry whether I might see him to give him information about the staff and my opinion of their capabilities and I had a discussion of some hours in which I put forward some of my own views on future prospects. I doubt if any of them that were sound had not already occurred to Sir William, but I was so deeply impressed by the new owners' straightforward friendliness that I felt an urge to pass on for what it was worth any knowledge I had of the paper. The immediate and very unexpected result was a letter the next morning asking whether I would accept the post of general manager. This I did with all the alacrity of a man who was whole-heartedly devoted to the paper and whose total income had in the twinkling of an eye been reduced to £6 14s. od. per annum as the holder of an infinitesimal share in one of the old *Daily Telegraph* trusts.

But as a result of this long conversation I was probably the first *Daily Telegraph* man to realize that Lord Camrose had bought the paper not as a vehicle for money-making, though he would be the first to admit that he was not allergic to profit, but because it represented more than any other daily paper his idea of what a good newspaper ought to be, an idea to which he had already given expression in his *Sunday Times*. He knew better than any of the would-be reformers on the staff what should be and what could be done. But he was as proud of *Daily Telegraph* tradition as any of its owners in its seventy years of life and as firm a believer in its ideas and ideals, though he took a more modern view of their proper implementation in a twentieth-century newspaper.

What Lord Camrose did for the *Daily Telegraph* is evidenced in its columns to-day. By his experience and judgment he guided it soundly. By his courage, energy, and enterprise he revitalized the collection and handling of news, and by his technical knowledge he modernized and improved the make-up. But he did something far more important to the life of a newspaper than these things, he gave back to the *Daily Telegraph* a belief in itself.

In its climb back, therefore, the paper had all that it wanted—a fine tradition, an honourable purpose, a good staff, an inspiring leader, and growing self-confidence. Success was certain though it must inevitably be of slow attainment. Pride is an essential of a successful newspaper and if it sometimes amounts to arrogance that is preferable to timidity. Camrose's *Telegraph* found the proper mean.

In that climb back, up to the separation of their interest, Lord Camrose was greatly helped on the business and advertising side by his brother. In no spirit of irreverence I would say that they were the most perfect double-turn that ever appeared on any stage and a pleasure to work with. Whether they ever had a difference of opinion on *Telegraph* matters I would not know. If they had, it must have been resolved so easily and instantaneously that no trace ever appeared.

If by force of circumstance I had to consult one on a matter previously discussed with the other I might have been resuming the conversation exactly where it had broken off. The building of newspapers in London apparently presents an easier problem to brothers than the building of walls in Rome.

The staff were as much surprised as the rest of Fleet Street were surprised at the fewness of the changes on the editorial side. Lord Camrose saw very clearly both the virtues and the failings of the *Telegraph*, and gradually and soundly he set out to strengthen the editorial staff in quality and quantity and to modernize its system of news collection.

He retained Arthur Watson as Editor until his retirement at the age of seventy in 1950. As Watson served for twenty-six years as Editor and saw the paper recover from a circulation of just under a hundred thousand to round about a million it is worth while examining the quality of the fifth Editor.

Watson had not the brilliance of Thornton Hunt or Edwin Arnold, but without the width of Le Sage's experience he had much of his supreme common sense. He had always the loyalty and affection of his staff and one inestimable virtue in the anxiety and rush of modern newspaper production that in no crisis of any kind, technical or political, did anyone see him in the slightest degree rattled.

In all the years I knew him I never asked him a question without getting a wise answer, not necessarily one with which I agreed, but nevertheless a wise answer. Watson owed a debt to Lord Camrose, similar to that of Le Sage to Edward Lawson, and is the first to acknowledge it. In the years from 1927 to 1950 the relations of Camrose and Watson were a model of relations between a working proprietor and his Editor. Camrose was not only proprietor but Editor-in-Chief of the paper. He brought to his task a considerable equipment, not only a knowledge of the world, organizing ability and business training, but a practical experience of editorial organization and control and newspaper production.

Here again was a case of *Daily Telegraph* history repeating itself. The first Lord Burnham had learned in the composing room. Lord Camrose had learned in the editorial chair and the less glamorous and less important editorial jobs which precede it. Both may have ended as financiers in the ignorant sense in which the word is used to describe those who happen to possess considerable means, but both were practical newspapermen who had come up the hard way and had made their money in the profession or industry in which they themselves laboured.

Lord Camrose exercised the political control of the paper and exercised it unquestionably and properly as an Editor-in-Chief should, and I doubt whether there was ever strong difference of opinion between him and Watson on political issues.

The energy and drive which went to the improvement of the editorial content of the paper and the scope of its news coverage were his. So, too, were the improvements in lay-out and display. Lord Camrose had an eye for type and a knowledge of typography which were sometimes tiresomely competent for some who thought they also knew something about it, and not least for the author of this history who incidentally would be the first to admit that Lord Camrose always not only appeared to be right but was in fact right.

In all these reformative years what impressed me most about Lord Camrose was not his knowledge which was extensive, nor his industry which was formidable, so much as his amazing courage in the expenditure of treasure for the benefit of the paper regardless of immediate advantage, and his complete confidence in his long-term policy.

The qualities of great men are those of intelligence and character or, put more crudely, brains and guts. Lord Camrose had plenty of both and I hope he realized what his inspiration meant to the members of his staff.

Unfortunately Viscount Burnham did not live to see a Balliol man appointed as Watson's successor. It would have given him a twofold pleasure to see Colin Coote's distinguished occupancy of the editorial chair and his loved paper forging past the million. He might have remembered that years back, when he was an undergraduate doubtful of the career, Jowett had sent him to the *Telegraph*. 'Your father owns a great newspaper. There is nothing to beat the job at hand. You must go to it.'

Coote is more in the Thornton Hunt-Arnold line than any of the previous three Editors though he is far more of an executive editor than probably Hunt or Arnold ever was. But he did not entirely abandon his pen when he moved from a small leader writer's room to the oak-panelled magnificence of the editorial apartment. Coote could rival Arnold for the speed in which he could master a subject and the polish of the finished article. Whether in a few hours he could write a poem as well as a leader may yet be revealed by a second Piper Findlater.

In the early years, Lord Camrose had the wise counsel of Lord Iliffe and the invaluable assistance of Lord Kemsley who organized and revitalized the advertisement department and interested himself specially in matters of circulation and management.

In making this distinction of function it should be said that it was not thus clearly defined. Nobody could say exactly how the brothers divided their work. It never seemed to worry them and therefore never caused any concern to anyone else in the office.

In 1937 the Triumvirate dissolved by agreement and its Caesar, Lord Camrose, took sole control of the *Daily Telegraph*. All was going well and when in the next year the crisis of Munich had passed he might have looked forward to an easier time.

Then in September, 1939, came the war. His two sons who had been associated with him in the direction and his general manager left to join their Territorial units and for six years he was left to bear the burden alone, and very manfully he discharged his task.

The story of the uninterrupted production of the *Daily Telegraph* in the war is one shared by all London newspapers. But for that it should have a long chapter to itself, in which it would be easy and very pleasant for a member of the staff who was not there, to record his admiration of and pride in all those who, through fire and high explosive and every imaginable lesser peril and inconvenience, never failed to get the paper out, and a very special note of tribute to the captain of the ship who had not only to face the risks of every action but all the problems of navigation. Critically important and difficult editorial decisions had to be made, and finance, shortages of raw material, and indeed every factor of production must have been one continual headache, but as the man who carried the burden never spoke about it this part of the book remains unwritten.

I find difficulty in concluding this chapter without the renewal of a puzzled wonderment as to how the *Daily Telegraph* not only survived but triumphed with its peculiar system or lack of system in management, how it tottered and how it recovered, and this inspires some possibly irrelevant thought as to what makes a successful newspaper.

The circulation of a newspaper is predominantly made editorially. Good distribution is a matter of mechanics requiring energy and attention to detail. Promotion requires vigour but presents no unusual problems of publicity, and once the circulation of the right kind and the right quantity is there it does not require a genius or a human dynamo to sell the advertising space. It is a complication that circulation, distribution, and revenue have to be built up simultaneously, made slightly easier in the last century when circulation income went further to meet total costs.

Every paper must have a definite editorial target of its own. Unless you have a very good and very clear idea of the sort of newspaper you want to produce you will never produce a good newspaper. At all costs you must avoid making your paper like the *Daily A.* or unlike the *Daily B.* because one appears to be successful, or the other either unsuccessful or the sort of paper you happen to dislike.

The morning post-mortem is very useful when it concerns your own paper but less so when it is conducted on your competitors, except to discover what you have wholly missed. What matters is your own judgment of whether a job is well done or not, uninfluenced by whether it may or may not be better done by someone else.

The exchange of early editions of other papers, at one time illicit and now recognized, produces the most fantastic results, and not infrequently the *Daily A.* puts down its own lead story in favour of the selection of the *Daily B.* and vice versa.

Intensive methods of promotion either by advertisement or the offer of adventitious attractions may put the paper into new hands, but readers will not be kept unless the paper gives them what they want, and the public still want news, though many of them may now be prepared to take it fairly scrappy and highly flavoured. But whatever your target your first and real problem is to get the paper right editorially and once you have decided your pattern you must go all out to reproduce it without evasion or reservation of any kind.

In the large amount of fragmentary material which

has been my source for the old days there is endless evidence of thought being given to the content of the paper and none to consideration of anything else.

The circumstances of the time did not require modern streamlined management and the chinks in the armour did not let in the shafts of the foeman till the arrival of Harmsworth's *Daily Mail*.

But though the system appeared incredibly loose and haphazard it worked much more effectively than its design would suggest. Though there may have been no very plain definition of function by title there was a very clear one by practice ; somebody looked after everything and everyone came to the boss for guidance, though neither Edward Lawson nor his father ever called himself either Editor or General Manager.

The least well organized department was the financial, which could never have survived ten minutes of the difficulties of present-day taxation and controls, but then it did not have to. It received what came in and paid out what it had to, leaving dividend policy to be settled by the patriarchs on grounds which in many years had little relation to financial or common sense. Replacements and developments could be looked after by the increased profits of the future and for a long time they were.

Advertising and circulation were cared for by subordinate commanders who did not carry many guns but fired what they had with considerable effect. Old whiskered E. T. Williamson whom I remember in the early nineteen-hundreds, and who had then held his office for some thirty years, was far from the modern concept of a circulation manager, and I am sure that his only predecessor, whose name even I cannot discover, was even less so. Yet this unremembered worthy cannot have been without talent. He was the first to put his paper on sale or return, and, though the decision must have been taken over his head, its implementation in those days must have needed a good ideal of practical ability. He was the first to organize special trains for distribution, now through co-operative arrangements at the Newspaper Proprietors' Association an essential feature of newspaper distribution.

The editorial staff was continually strengthened in numbers and authority as the paper grew in stature. Of the men in other departments one might say that the paper's progress outgrew their ability and that they remained small men in what became big jobs. But they served loyally and well and the proprietors' affection for old faces did them no harm until the whole tempo of competition changed.

The overwhelming circulation of the eighties, the unquestioned authority and popularity of the paper and its remarkable prosperity were not achieved by ' duds ' in any department. These men on the business side may not have been what we would now call high-powered, they had no degrees, certificates or diplomas, they had learned their jobs by the method by which Wackford Squeers taught spelling, but in their funny old way they got results.

Nothing and nobody outside the editorial department got proper attention up to the twentieth century and Lord Camrose and his associates had plenty to do to modernize and man the machine.

For his editorial directive Lord Camrose departed little from Thornton Hunt's advice to his chief which I have recorded in the first chapter and from various other proprietorial instructions given since, and that not because he was unoriginal, no one less, but because these express the unchanging requirement of a good newspaper for thinking men and women.

A good newspaper for thinking men and women has always been the aim of *Daily Telegraph* proprietors.

Because Lord Camrose never lost sight of that objective and was able to recreate the imagination, spirit and drive of the pioneers, what they had raised from a circulation of a few hundred to three hundred thousand he was able to bring from ninety thousand to over the million.

CHAPTER XV

ADVENTURE BRAVE AND NEW

OF my two architects of *Daily Telegraph* success the first, Edward Lord Burnham, is remembered by those, who though much younger, knew him mainly as a friend and a host. There are very few left who worked with him and then only when he was in partial retirement, and they, in lesser occupations than those which they subsequently filled, had slight personal contact with him. The records of his earlier colleagues, though universally expressing deep admiration for his ability and affection for him as a man, give little detail of his life and work. It is the pious hope of the author that something of his genius and of his generous and friendly self appears in the pages of this book. It can be fairly said that the *Daily Telegraph* is his memorial, though he may share that memorial with another.

With my second architect, William Viscount Camrose, it is very different. My difficulty is rather that there are so many who knew him well and his vital personality is so fresh in memory that I do not know what to write and what to leave unwritten.

I do not try, therefore, to describe his manifold achievements in the newspaper world outside the *Telegraph* or in any other directions. This is the story of the *Daily Telegraph* and not of any individual.

But his particular achievement in bringing back the past glory of the *Telegraph* and adding to it a new lustre is of such importance and interest that this book, though it gives no more than impressionistic sketches of the great men of the *Telegraph*, must attempt that most difficult of tasks, the portrait of a man whom all who see it knew.

It is the work of two artists, his Editor and his General Manager, and it endeavours to show him at work—with a background illustrating something of the task which he had in hand. Like many portraits it fails to convey the essential greatness of the subject but its contemporariness, with its difficulties, carries the consolation that at any rate for a very long time he will be judged by the memory of my readers and not by my poor use of words.

Arthur Watson, who served him as Editor for all but four years of his *Daily Telegraph* life, very willingly agreed to do what I asked of him and I am grateful to him for contributing something which no one could do as well as he. My previous chapter was written before I planned this one and altogether independently we make some of the same observations about the change and record the same opinions of our new master. Two witnesses are better than one and I have left these comments uncut and unaltered.

*   *   *   *   *

Watson writes:

I first met Lord Camrose (then Sir William Berry) in the last days of December, 1927, when I had been Editor of the *Daily Telegraph* under Viscount Burnham for three years. The paper had some days before carried the announcement of its purchase by Sir William, his brother Gomer, and Sir Edward Iliffe, then combined in a partnership that was later dissolved, and the news had not been very well received either in the *Daily Telegraph* offices or in ' The Street ' outside. Not a great deal was known about the Berry brothers except that they had bought some important papers, mostly in the North of England, and it was too hastily assumed—in the light of some recent experiences which had made Fleet Street very sensitive—that this was another case of outside interests coming into a business of which they had no knowledge, with probably adverse effects upon staffs, and perhaps upon the papers. It was true that the Berry brothers had owned the *Sunday Times* for some dozen years, but it was not generally appreciated how much the improvement in that paper and the progress it was making were due to their personal and tireless handling, and to the long hours that Sir William spent in the office each Saturday, imprinting throughout that night's issue his convictions of what a Sunday paper should be.

On the night the purchase was announced, the Editor of another paper who had had some difficult experiences of the kind rang me up in search of further information. None was forthcoming, and he went on roundly to denounce financiers who bought up newspapers, but he finished by saying: ' Mind, I don't say that about Bill Berry; he is one of the best.'

For my part, I became worried about the staff, knowing that they were themselves worried about the future. I had been careful to tell them the news before there was any possibility of their hearing it from outside the office, but it was not long before men whom I was anxious not to lose began to trickle into my room with gloomy apprehensions of extensive changes on the paper. The actual transfer of ownership was not to take place immediately, and I feared a drift away to other papers. It was a good staff, most of the members very carefully hand-picked, as they always have been, and I knew that to build up again in the same quality would be the work of years.

I therefore sought an interview with Sir William Berry at his office in Arundel Street, and told him that the staff was getting restless. I found him completely understanding. In the quiet straightforward way with which I later became familiar, he assured me, ' There is nobody whom I wish to get on the *Daily Telegraph*, and there is nobody on the *Daily Telegraph* of whom I wish to get rid.' It subsequently became clear that this statement was as true as it was precise.

On January 9th, 1928, Sir William Berry and his brother took over direction. It was with Sir William, who made himself responsible for the editorial side of the paper, that I mostly came into contact—and the contact was daily. It quickly became apparent that he had not come into control as a financier, but as a journalist, and a journalist of the first quality. I am quite sure that he took more delight in forging the paper as he thought it ought to be than in its commercial success; but he would not have thought his editorial work to have been well done—and, indeed, it could not have been continued at all—had not financial success accompanied it. I watched the sequence with interest. First, the paper must be of a high order; that is to say, tempting to look at and satisfying when read. Secondly, circulation must be built up on editorial merit. Thirdly, an advertisement campaign could be successfully based on wider circulation.

Sir William had very definite ideas about what he wanted in a newspaper, and the clearest possible views about what he did not want.

Of the basic character of the *Daily Telegraph* he approved. That was no doubt why he bought it, for he was a man who considered his courses long and carefully. He therefore desired no revolutionary changes. But it is not too much to say that the virtues of the *Telegraph* were at that time of a rather negative quality; they derived from restraint rather than from vigour. Of its weaknesses the staff had been extremely conscious, but they could do nothing about it. They of necessity danced to the tune that was played. The existing control had been too parsimonious; there were too many advertisements and not enough news and features. No paper, it may be said, can have too many advertisements. That is in a sense true, but there was a lack of balance. Sir William Berry did not hesitate to redress it from the very first day by increasing the number of pages, for which there was not at that time any compensating increase in advertisements.

Through a daily appraisal of the contents he very quietly but positively instilled the policy he wished to be followed. ' Quality ' was from the first his guiding principle. There must be no sensationalism of any kind. The news service must be extended and still of the highest quality. It meant considerable additions to the editorial costs, but Sir William was prepared to find the money.

The greater freedom which increased space allowed was felt immediately. Under the old régime we had always struggled to print readers' letters, expressing a point of view different from the paper's own, but, working in a strait jacket, we were rarely able to find space for more than one or two. In the new conditions, with more pages at disposal, two inviolable columns were set aside every day for letters to the Editor. Similarly, pictures were given adequate space without curtailing the news. Gradually, very gradually, the face of the paper began to change. While still devoted to solid news, it became more sprightly and gave confidence for the successful reduction of price from twopence to a penny. Some years later, on one spectacular day before the war, the paper appeared in more modern form with news on the front page instead of an unbroken array of small advertisements. It was not a pioneering change, but in the circumstances of the *Telegraph* it was not an easy one, for it involved much explanation to various classes of advertisers who claimed a traditional right to the reader's first glance. There was, however, never any doubt that the step was a wise one. It definitely marked the transition from the old order to the new, and the circulation climbed to three-quarters of a million by the outbreak of war.

It is a remarkable fact—and amongst other things a sidelight on Lord Camrose's character—that this resurgence into prosperity was able to be effected with the old staff, with no more changes than time will always bring.

I have already said that it was a good staff that Lord Camrose took over. The organization, too, was much better than it had been a few years before. The opportunity of Sir John Le Sage's retirement had been taken to introduce the post of news editor, something the *Daily Telegraph* had never had in the full sense of the term. Sir John had combined the work of news editor with his editorship, which had been possible in his earlier days but had long since become quite incompatible with efficiency. The result was that the paper had become far more dependent upon the news agencies than a leading paper ought to be.

It was once said that the *Daily Telegraph* grows its own men. The man for the new post was indeed ready to hand. It was given, almost as a matter of course, to W. T. Massey. Massey had been on the paper a good many years and his experience embraced many fields. He had worked in Parliament, was familiar with the law courts, and he was described to me by another outstanding journalist, Stephen Glanville (of whom more later), as the best sub-editor he had ever known. He had been in Northern Ireland during the troubles there; he had covered the more important events at home, and he had travelled widely abroad in the service of the paper. In the early days of the First World War he had acted as a correspondent in France, and later he had represented the whole of the London Press with Allenby's army in Palestine. A very distinguished special correspondent, Perceval Landon, whose *Daily Telegraph* career was terminated by a premature death, told me that wherever he went in the world he found the trail of Massey, and it was associated in local minds with such personal memories that it always made things easier for him. That was a very fine compliment from one correspondent to another.

Add to this full life a cool, common-sense brain, and there were all the qualifications of an informed and wide-awake news editor, capable of extending and maintaining at a peak of efficiency both home and foreign services, as Massey did for many years.

It was the news editor's business to gather material for the paper, and to see that nothing was missing from the record of the day's events. It was for others to find a place for it in the paper; to discard, compress, and in the final resort to discard again. That was for the night staff, and the chief responsibility fell on Stephen Glanville, with Arthur Rowe as his chief sub-editor and right-hand man.

Glanville had served for many years on the *Telegraph* staff, but had left to become Editor of the *Shipping Gazette and Lloyd's List* when the Committee of Lloyds had decided to develop this as a more general newspaper. That policy was reversed about the time that I had been put into the Editor's chair, and the opportunity was taken to tempt Glanville back to Peterborough Court. He was a man of quick, incisive mind, full of good humour, but with an acid tongue which came explosively into play at any sign of inefficiency. His reappearance added the strength of a man whose judgment and energy could be relied upon.

It was a matter of regret when, some years after the change of ownership, both Massey and Glanville reached the age of retirement. By that time, however, new men had come along. Eric Stowell had joined the paper from Manchester and was destined to play a leading part in its news management. The acquisition of the *Morning Post* brought a new accession of capable journalists. When I joined the staff it consisted largely of young men, but it had tended to age. Now it became young again. Two leader writers came from the *Morning Post*. Robert Hield was a gallant veteran, with a graceful pen inspired by an impressively wide knowledge, but J. C. Johnstone was young and had special contacts with economic and industrial circles. S. R. Pawley, another young man, strengthened the news side and became foreign editor after the war, and G. C. Hepburn-Reid, who followed after an interval, ultimately became editor of the Manchester edition.

Lord Camrose was from the first insistent upon a wide news coverage by his own staff, regardless of cost, and as the paper prospered, so the staff and the expenses increased. To watch the matter more closely, he had a news tape machine on his own floor, and he was frequently in touch with the news editor over the office telephone to know what was being done. Gradually contact was widened with local correspondents throughout the country, so that a report could be readily obtained or expanded at any time, and the news agencies were less relied upon. The *Daily Telegraph* had a tradition of strength on the foreign side, with a body of resident correspondents in all-important centres familiar with the language and conditions of the country they represented, but the net was cast still wider and its meshes were smaller.

The link between the proprietorship and those who carried out its policy had always been an intimate one on the *Telegraph*, and it continued so under the new conditions. Men were working for a personality, sitting in the same office and in constant touch, whose professional wisdom and knowledge of affairs they quickly came to respect. I suppose there was never a more inquiring mind than that of Lord Camrose. A reporter would come back with what he believed to be a complete answer to some question raised by him, only to be met by a new set of penetrating queries which sent him out again with the feeling that he had hardly pierced the surface of his subject. It made for a wholesome faith in the direction of the paper and a standard of work which built up confidence between proprietor and staff.

My own relations with my chief were always good, if not always completely smooth. We had a conference every midday, in which the good deeds and misdeeds of that morning were discussed, as well as plans for the future. But there was an earlier contact than that. As journalists must, Lord Camrose tackled his newspapers in his first waking moments, and he had a secretary at his house early, to whom he dictated his criticisms and suggestions for transmission to the office. The terms, in the freshness of the morning, were apt to be a little rasping, but it usually happened, when I saw him an hour or two later, that while the criticisms remained the testiness had gone.

The custom was for us to meet again in the afternoon or early evening, when the leader subjects were chosen or those confirmed which had already been arranged. Difficulties did not often arise here, but at time of stirring events, at home or abroad, these discussions were apt to be protracted, and on those occasions a leader writer would be called in for additional counsel.

From what I have said, some indication will have been

gleaned of the sort of man Lord Camrose was. Perhaps I may elaborate the picture. Physically he was tall, clean-shaven, good-looking, straight in the back and in the eye, soft-spoken, and with a quiet geniality which quickly made him popular. On close acquaintance you were struck by the directness and lucidity of his speech and the certainty with which he knew his own mind. While conservative by nature, he retained a freedom of outlook and a capacity for original action in a new situation which frequently took his subordinates completely by surprise. He liked to keep everything in his own hands; but he judged his men and would go away without warning in the confidence that those he had nursed but yet trusted would carry on competently in his absence. In the daily round he could be relied on to give a quick decision—and who would not value that as a very high quality in his chief?—but he liked time to consider his problems, and when his decision had been taken he made no concession of time to anyone who had to carry it out. He relied on his own judgment and could rarely be moved. His justification was that he was almost invariably right, and he was generally proved right when I and others believed him to be wrong. If, on rare occasion, he made a mistake, he put the blame on no one but himself. He was extremely generous to anyone in difficulty or distress, and extremely human in his personal dealings. Outside the office he had wide interests and a large circle of friends—assets of great importance to a journalist. In all he did he was scrupulously honest and laboriously just.

I cannot close without a word about the war years. They were difficult years for everybody and brought special problems to newspapers, which were deprived of most of their raw material—newsprint. Before the war Lord Camrose had brought his eldest son, Seymour (the present Lord Camrose), into the office. Like his father, and like most London journalists, he had received his early newspaper training in the provinces, and he was taking part in the control. On the outbreak of war he joined his Territorial regiment, as did the General Manager and many of the staff. Lord Camrose sat alone in the proprietorial rooms, contemptuous of air-raid warnings, wrestling with the problem, as Government restrictions closed down upon Fleet Street, of preserving the special character of the *Daily Telegraph* in face of an order to cut down to four pages. To strengthen his case he increased the price to three-halfpence, against the penny at which the 'popular' papers were sold, and fought tenaciously for the right to print six pages most of the week, with an occasional four. He won, but only at the cost of some 180,000 copies daily to bring the consumption of newsprint within the ration. It was a hard necessity, but in the continued differentiation of the paper from others, a springboard was preserved for return to its own sphere when opportunity came. Lord Camrose found relief from anxieties in personal dealing with ever more detail, till with the return of peace his resilient, but industrious, optimism was matched by a circulation soaring to a million copies in freer but still restricted conditions.

All those who worked with him through that difficult period and the previous strenuous years of building will think of him, as I do, with affection and admiration.

* * * * *

Arthur Watson's task to expand his staff and develop his news services was no less great than mine, but in some ways easier in that it could be achieved more gradually.

Lord Camrose's first outline of his hopes and plans left me in no doubt that for some time I should have so much to do with rebuilding and re-equipping as to have

196

little time for any of the other problems of management. Such of those problems as affected the editorial side were tackled by Lord Camrose with Watson, and Lord Kemsley undertook the reorganization of the advertising department. Circulation promotion had to be invigorated but there was no question of any out and out drive until the product was ready.

The first two things in Lord Camrose's mind were his editorial development and the change of his page size to what is now accepted as the standard size of a newspaper. (The old *Telegraph* page was two and a half inches longer.)

With this last requirement he said that his machine room must be capable of printing up to forty-page papers against the then limit of twenty-four and eight pages more than the capacity of any national newspaper, and further of course that they must be capable of a far higher production. He and I have sometimes argued since as to what he then wanted in numbers. I cannot remember what it was but I am sure that it was less than he ultimately got and more than I suggested to be necessary.

Editorial expansion demanded the rebuilding of the front office which housed the editorial staff and which was already filled to capacity. That was the easiest part of the problem. The sale of the *Daily Telegraph*, besides bringing about many more important changes, healed a three-generation-old feud between my great-grandfather and the optical firm of Troughton and Simms by which their shop next door to the *Telegraph* was never allowed to pass into the hands of the Lawson family, and the second building to the west happened to be owned by Lord Iliffe.

There was, therefore, new ground to build on and use until the old front office could be pulled down and the new building completed. Lord Iliffe was entrusted by his co-proprietors with this matter and W. E. Elcock of the firm of Elcock and Sutcliffe was the architect.

The ideal internal lay-out could not be achieved because of the necessity of building in two halves. The façade speaks for itself and the internal planning was reasonably satisfactory and sufficiently elastic to be capable of later readjustments.

The mechanical side was a headache. The large island site at the back surrounded by narrow passages had only a single egress to Fleet Street and was filled by a factory building of super-solid construction. The publishing room had been overloaded by a production of a quarter of a million of a twenty-page paper, and the presses had found difficulty in producing the same number of any paper requiring three units, i.e. twenty-four pages (each unit of a press produces eight pages).

It looked as if the only thing to do would be to find alternative accommodation and plant during reconstruction and re-equipment of the old establishment, but nothing suitable was available. The factory building, like Topsy, had grown and was fairly complicated. About the second time we tramped it Lord Camrose said, ' At any rate I seem to have got the only man who knows his way about the whole of this building.' He was good enough to record that opinion in his book.

After a good deal of discussion he agreed to a general plan and a vast expenditure and left me to get on with the job. He was an admirably decisive and pleasant man to work for.

The first paper of the new size appeared just over two years after the new proprietors had assumed control. In the meanwhile its appearance like its content had not remained unaltered. There was much more white space, double-column openings, the news was generally better displayed and there were many typographical improvements. Advertising revenue was considerably higher and the advertising was more varied and attractive. More revolutionary changes were the reduction of the selling price to one penny and, very much later, news on the front page.

When I had my first long meeting with Lord Camrose before he gave me a job I had stressed the handicap of our selling price. My argument was that our place was between *The Times* and the 'populars' but our price must be competitive with the mass circulation newspapers.

Heaven knows Lord Camrose was active enough in those days and kept his lieutenants active enough, but I sometimes felt impatient at his delayed action on the selling price. He was of course much wiser than I and realized that he was in a position to back it each way. If he could make a success of it at twopence it would be gratifying, and if he could not he would at any rate have the advantage of not making this all-important change until he was fully equipped to take advantage of it. The paper was not ready for a greatly increased circulation.

If I had expressed my impatience at his not making his full effort sooner he might well have replied, as did Fred Archer when asked why he did not come earlier, that he could not come without the horse.

On Saturday, February 15th, 1930, the *Daily Telegraph* came out in the old size, and from the same composing room, foundry, and machine room on Monday, February 17th, in the new size. Hectic would be a mild description of the intervening forty-eight hours. Had I not been aware that all the credit, except for a little thinking and planning, was due to the works manager, head printer, overseers, and the whole of the mechanical staff I should have been inordinately pleased with myself. Lord Camrose was generously appreciative of the efforts of everybody.

This change was made the subject of a leader which

in the peroration recalled something of the old floridity. It began, ' The *Daily Telegraph* appears to-day in a new dress.' Some technical detail follows ending with the statement that ' The day of the tall newspaper, as of the tall folio, is gone '. Then came some of the advantages of the new size ending up with

> It is for these reasons the *Daily Telegraph* has spent £200,000 on gigantic printing presses [this was for the machinery alone without the cost of the structural changes] of the latest pattern each able to print a forty-page paper at the rate of forty thousand copies an hour, and hence the new dress of a journal which has always striven honourably to lead the way and stand among the foremost, unsworn to the service of any person or Party, unaddicted to extremes, and the friend of ordered liberty and progress.

J. B. Firth, who wrote it, was well capable of looking up what Thornton Hunt had written for another launching. I doubt if he did, but there is a faint echo of the fanfare of 1855.

At the end of the same year, on December 1st, the price was reduced to a penny. The earlier changes had arrested the fall in circulation and started an increase, but it was still a little under a hundred thousand.

Lord Camrose was conscious of the importance of this change and made it the subject of his first personal pronouncement in the paper. First he referred to the circumstances of his taking over control and then wrote of the various improvements in newsprint, typography, and general readability. He went on:

> But the policy of the paper remains unchanged. It is, as it always had been, the aim of the *Daily Telegraph* to chronicle the events of the day succinctly and fairly, to comment without misrepresentation, and to keep the reader abreast of the literary, scientific, and artistic movements of the time.

The literary form was different from the turgid and sententious pronouncements of 1855 but the intention was the same.

Of opinion he wrote:

> Politically the *Daily Telegraph* is in close sympathy with the policy of the Conservative Party and believes that the problems with which the country and the Empire are confronted to-day will best be served by that policy. It is hardly necessary to state that it has no official or financial connection with any Party and, as its old readers know, it does not hesitate to express an independent view when the circumstances warrant it.

The early fathers had been too uncertain of their political allegiance to claim more, or less, than to be ' champions of the people and advocates of measures of general progress which they believe to be for the good of the people '. Lord Camrose ended his article by making very clear that the change was one of price only and not of character. In the book which he wrote many years later he records that there was no difference except price in the twopenny paper on Saturday and the penny paper on the Monday. Nevertheless the circulation doubled itself in a week.

Naturally I said to myself, ' How damned well right I was in what I said in Arundel Street three years ago.' If I had then given it a tenth of the thought which I have given it since I would have added, ' And how damned well he knew exactly what he was doing.' What sort of a job could we have made of the change of size if the circulation had been a quarter of a million or more instead of a hundred thousand?

The transition of editorial and managerial offices was not nearly so difficult, if slightly uncomfortable. It was made easier by the fact that Lord Camrose had bought the old *Westminster Gazette* building which adjoined our printing works and was made intercommunicating with them.

The work was completed in two halves. For some months we lived in rather faded Victorian splendour with a scaffolding-filled gap to the west of us, and for further months in neo-Georgian magnificence with a scaffolding-filled gap to the east.

The new Fleet Street building was completed at the end of 1929 and Lord Camrose, Lord Kemsley and Lord Iliffe were able to move in, and the considerably increased editorial staff had elbow room.

With his own secretariat and the editorial staff of the *Telegraph* at hand he was able to give the paper all the attention that he wanted to. At that time he still had very considerable other newspaper responsibilities. Certainly not financially, and indeed in no respect except mentally, was the *Telegraph* his chief interest. From then on he could more easily devote to the *Telegraph* the full force of his imagination, knowledge, and drive.

What sort of a man was he to work for? I feel that in this record I should do more than give the simple answer ' Grand '.

First his shortcomings, or at any rate what for a servant fell short of perfection in his master. Like all newspaper proprietors I have served or known he had a tendency to want to dig up the plant just a little too often to see how it was growing. But to wish to do that (if not to do it) is a fault of some of the best gardeners.

He did not always maintain a perfect observance of what I should have called in one of my other metamorphoses ' staff duties ', or at any rate he would not let such considerations cramp his style. He was so keen that he would sometimes do something that was part of your job and forget to let you know about it. If he found out that it had caused any difficulty he would put it right with a few words and a laugh. He was deeply appreciative of anything that was done for him or for the paper but sometimes found a curious difficulty in expressing it, due to a certain shyness which is sometimes found in decisive and forthright men.

Once he had given you a job to do he left you to do it and gave you your instructions with admirable clarity and economy of words. If it was done wrongly he told you so in unmistakable terms but very agreeably. He had a quick temper which was seldom shown and passed with extraordinary rapidity. I made many mistakes while I worked under his direction but never the same one twice and in so far as I know my job he taught me about seventy-five per cent of it. He was immensely competent, enthusiastic, generous in mind and deed, exacting, just, and fun to work with and for. I have served many men but can remember no other of whom I have no single unfavourable recollection. For that alone I would be glad to serve his successors until incipient senility shows clearer signs than I hope it does to-day. That service is made easier and more agreeable by their pleasing personalities, the quick mind and flair of Seymour the second Lord Camrose, our new Chairman, and the fine brain and devotion to work of his brother Michael, our new Editor-in-Chief.

From 1930 on the story is one of uninterrupted progress, except for the artificial ups and downs of wartime circulation which I have dealt with elsewhere. The events of the last twenty years and the *Daily Telegraph* treatment of them are too fresh in memory for detailed record in this book. The events were the most serious of the nation's history, but every reader has lived through them and I will not recall their experience.

When the paper reached a million sale Lord Camrose reviewed its accomplishment and its future in a long leader-page article.

By the side of the ' big battalion ' sales of the popular dailies the *Daily Telegraph* figure of a million seems a comparatively small total. But surely it is a healthy sign of the times that a paper of its character should make solid progress against the more sensational note of some of its contemporaries. Obviously the contents of the paper do not make such a wide appeal as those of the newspapers which seek to entertain more than to inform. They never can do so. Neither is the manner in which the news is presented calculated to attract sensation-loving minds.

On the other hand the *Daily Telegraph* has proved that there is a consistently growing section of the public which appreciates a paper aiming to be of steady balanced character, and which, while vigilant in enterprise, does not try to distort news or views to sensational ends. That is the standard of journalism we have set out to achieve, and it is always for our readers to decide how far we have maintained it.

He went on to regret that newsprint shortage prevented as much attention as he would like to be given to affairs of national and world importance, and then apologetically reviewed what he called 'the parochial question of advertising'. Finally he stated his faith and made his testament. 'Never under my control will the paper change its character in an attempt to force a rapid increase in the number of its readers.'

Some newspapers to-day have created trusts, intended to ensure that the future ownership and control shall not pass into the hands of undesirable proprietors who might change the character of the papers. I do not feel that such legal instruments are necessary or that they will achieve their purpose. So far as the *Daily Telegraph* is concerned I have already taken what I regard as effective measures to perpetuate the paper in its present form, so far as that can ever be achieved, by handing over the voting control to my two elder sons (Mr. Seymour Berry and Mr. Michael Berry) who, except for the years of the war, have been in journalism all their adult lives. I have retained the Chairmanship for my lifetime, or for so long as I choose to occupy that position, and I feel that mine is a more realistic policy than that of leaving the last word in the hands of inexperienced people, however distinguished they may be.

The ' young professionals ' are ably carrying on the control, Seymour as Chairman and Michael as Editor-in-Chief, and the more easily because they find that paternal piety coincides with their natural talent and inclination.

CHAPTER XVI

THANKS A MILLION

THE story is told that a certain Cairo jeweller attained great wealth and, incidentally, the rank of Pasha and a hundred years of age. Shortly after the last leg of his triple achievement someone meeting one of his sons said 'votre père est centenaire, n'est ce pas', to which the son answered—'non, millionaire'.

The *Daily Telegraph* is now both centenaire and millionaire. A hundred years old and a circulation of a million without showing overweening pride or crippling senility.

Lord Camrose took over the *Daily Telegraph* with a circulation of under 100,000 daily. Considerable speculation was aroused in Fleet Street on two points, first of all whether he would be able to re-establish the *Telegraph* at all, and secondly what was the ceiling of a 'quality' newspaper.

The first doubt was soon resolved. Deliberately at the start progress was slow. Lord Camrose did not reduce the selling price to a penny until 1930 because, although he was ready to shoot hard, he did not want his weapon to go off at half-cock. Many of his improvements, and particularly those that were editorial, could be put into operation fairly rapidly. The provision of accommodation for an expanded staff and the installation of new plant to make the paper of a more acceptable size, and typographical and other technical improvements inevitably required time.

But by the end of 1930 the circulation was over 175,000 and steadily increasing. In another eighteen months the figure was probably the highest ever. One cannot be certain about that because the records of the previous century are not as reliable as the chartered accountants' certificates of to-day.

The first answer was clear. Nothing short of national disaster could stop the *Telegraph*, and in seven years national disaster came and could not. The second question was far more interesting and continues to arouse speculation. It is easy to write the prescription for a 'quality' newspaper though it may be harder to make it up—to be comprehensive without being voluminous, to be serious without being dull, to be bright without being trivial, to be instructive without being didactic, to be fair-minded without being irresolute. But even when and if this ideal can be attained there is still the further point to be decided of what is the extent of the field for a newspaper of that kind.

The growth of public education somehow or other has not produced a corresponding growth of serious interest in public affairs or a desire for thorough and accurate information. Who doubts this had better take a look at the largest circulations of to-day. No names, no pack drill.

There is a further limiting factor. The Parliamentary system of this country is a two-party one and any newspaper which hopes to be constructive must generally align itself with the policy of one of them and so deny itself the readership of the most ardent supporters of the other. This argument does not presume that all the readers of the *Daily Telegraph* are Tories any more than that all the readers of the *Daily Mirror* are Socialists, but the effect of party loyalty on circulation is sensible.

Even in the office, various ceilings were suggested for the *Daily Telegraph*. Some of us would now hate to be reminded of our stated opinions, some are still waiting to be proved right.

Early in 1935 the 400,000 was reached and by the end of the following year a steady half million. By the beginning of the war it was 750,000 and then all speculation ceased because natural growth gave way to every sort of artificial influence.

Before we consider war-time circulation it is worth examining the truly remarkable achievement of a decade. Most of us have forgotten the circumstances of Fleet Street between the wars, and those who remember do so with distaste. They were the most discreditable in the history of newspaper rivalry. The mass circulation newspapers were violently engaged in a cut-throat battle to promote their sales by every adventitious aid to circulation imaginable, insurance, free gifts, large prize competitions—everything which the ingenuity and enterprise of managements could devise, except the perfection of the literary content.

We sat in no ivory tower. We did not delude ourselves that however superior we, at least, thought our own paper to be, the acquiring of a mangle or a set of cooking utensils was not an attraction to the housewife, or a set of bound volumes to her husband. After all, they did not have to read the paper for more than a comparatively short period, and the temporary effect on the sales of those who gave away nothing but only sold a newspaper was not entirely negligible.

Nevertheless Lord Camrose was resolutely determined to sell his paper on its intrinsic merit, in the trenchant phrase in which I have heard him crystallize his thought ' no cigars or nuts ', and he saw his three-quarters of a million by the time war broke out.

The changes of the next six years were too unreal to justify detailed record. Perhaps the most courageous and significant decision made by Lord Camrose was in

1941 when he decided to sacrifice some hundred thousand of sale in order to be able to give more pages daily.

It must have been very tempting, when advertising revenue was scanty, to take the extra sales and have the larger circulation in hand for expansion when the war came to an end, but a very long-sighted man took the view that what really mattered was to preserve the character of the *Daily Telegraph*, and that he could not give the public what he felt they had a right to expect from the *Telegraph* on four pages every day.

Newsprint rationing found many forms, by tonnage, by paging, by limitation to the average circulation of a reference period and so on. The first time any sort of normality returned was in September 1946, and how great had been the restraint on the *Telegraph's* natural growth was shown by an immediate increase of over a hundred thousand. In seven months' time, in April, the million was reached for the first time and held for three months.

Then restrictions were reimposed and remained in force until January 1949. These had the effect of reducing the circulations to just over 900,000. For those in newspaper board-rooms and circulation departments it was like living in a mad house, but Lord Camrose did not show any consciousness of it. Throughout he showed a serene confidence that all this gallimaufry of control was incidental and temporary and did not matter much. He had become enthusiastic when he got his million, and when it was taken away from him he never doubted that he would get it again as soon as he was allowed to.

Sales were freed in January 1949, but only for just over a year and a half in which we got eighty thousand back towards the million, and then back came limitations which did not in fact reduce circulation but froze it, and frozen it remained until October 1952.

Less than a year saw us then back to a million in March 1953.

This rather involved story of war-time difficulties is only given to explain the obstacles in the natural march to the million.

Of course a million is not the ceiling, it is only a landing on the stairway. How far the staircase may extend cannot be known, for it is built as we go along. There is something of the Indian rope trick in all newspaper progress.

So far the author has attempted in the record of events to be as objective as possible and in the assessment of actions, policies, and individuals to conceal none of the chinks in the armour. He now feels that through its historian the *Daily Telegraph* may be permitted to indulge in a little unadulterated self-esteem. Those who were not, as he, practically born and bred in the office cannot be expected to derive the same satisfaction at its success and the same hopes of its prospects. Those who do not think that it is in any way remarkable as a newspaper will probably not have read this book. To those who are in any way doubtful about its claims I would suggest that the attainment of a sale of over a million copies daily by a newspaper of this kind is not only an exceptional achievement in newspaper history, but also gives encouraging thought to the sociologist. So much is done to-day to obviate the necessity of thinking of any kind, to titillate the palate of the newspaper reader with highly spiced material, that it must be comforting to think that so many people of both sexes and all ages will every day buy a newspaper which, whatever its faults of omission and commission, and they are many, can only appeal to those who are reasonably serious-minded and who take a responsible view of the importance of being well informed on things that really matter.

And perhaps the author might be excused a personal

note. I would not know what my grandfather had in mind when he first entered the composing room or the editorial office of the paper which his family had acquired in such peculiar circumstances. Possibly he had no deeper thought than that it was a great opportunity for a young man of spirit who had been apprenticed to the printing trade.

He learned much from his brilliant writers and thinkers, from Thornton Hunt and from Edwin Arnold. He paid attention to his wise counsellors like Edward Dicey and Iwan Muller. Le Sage gave him not only his unfailing assistance but a share of his knowledge of the technique of the job.

Just as quickly and as thoroughly he got a conception of the importance of the job itself, a vision of the potentiality of a great newspaper conducted on high standards, and the rapidity of the change from the circulation-catching methods of the early years was very notable. Probably he never changed in his ideas, though in the early years he was not firmly enough established to control his own enthusiasts, nor perhaps was he above turning the blind eye to much that was in need of the blue pencil. His ideal was fixed and he saw his purpose very clearly. He wanted his paper to be popular but above all he wanted it to be trusted and respected. I never saw him at work at the office, but I often heard him in his little room at Hall Barn discuss the paper over his private telephone. The meticulousness of his care to see that his leading articles were responsible and constructive was amazing.

His son was indeed fortunate to find a new proprietor with the same high concept, the same thorough knowledge of the job, the same courage in the adventure of newspaper building, and the same freshness of thought and energy in its translation into action.

I am fully aware that as an author I am wide open to

the charge of prejudice in favour of my grandfather and my boss. I have for both the greatest affection and admiration which I honestly believe to be short of idolatry. What I would most firmly maintain is that anyone who has read these pages or studied themselves the history of the *Daily Telegraph* would freely admit that this book is rightly dedicated to these two men as the architects of success.

How great their success may have been, or whether their journey in its attainment was really necessary, can only be judged by studying the record and taking a look at the *Daily Telegraph* as it is to-day.

During my service as General Manager at intervals I received inquiries from readers asking for an explanation of the device and motto which appears above the leaders. These I was unable to satisfy until quite recently when, rummaging through some old papers at home, I found the answer.

They come from a suggestion for a coat of arms sent by the College of Heralds to my grandfather at some time when the parvenu printers first began to take an interest in the peculiar customs of the aristocracy. He did not accept it for his personal use but must have thought that the design of telegraph poles and the wings of Hermes was suitable for a newspaper.

So too was the motto for a paper thirty years old, with pride in its present, and confidence in its future. So without, so far as I know, permission from or acknowledgement to the College he appropriated it for his leader column.

'Was, is and will be.' The *Daily Telegraph's* past I have attempted to record, of its present you must judge for yourselves, for its future neither Lord Camrose would have wished, nor his sons or anyone in Peterborough Court would ask, more than that it should flourish as much and for as long as it deserves.

INDEX

INDEX

World War, First, reporting in, 69–70, 103, 192; Lansdowne Letter in, 154–60
World War, Second, 181; reporting in, 71–2, 74; *Telegraph* in, 208–9
Wortham, Hugo, 126

Y
Yates, Edmund, 6, 48

Year's Art, The, 124
Yellow Book, 95
Yellow Peril, 152
Yorkshire Post, 156

Z
Zola, Emile, 147
Zulu War, 69, 96